THE SECRETS I KEPT

Kiva McClendon Crutcher

Copyright © 2024 Kiva McClendon Crutcher
All rights reserved
First Edition

Fulton Books
Meadville, PA

Published by Fulton Books 2024

ISBN 979-8-88982-595-1 (paperback)
ISBN 979-8-88982-596-8 (digital)

Printed in the United States of America

MY SECRETS KEPT ME SICK

After many years in recovery, I decided to write my story! Not just to rid some of my unresolved issues about the past but to also contribute to the healing process of others that may be suffering from their own personal traumas and may be living with shame and guilt. I also wanted to share how God delivered me as He provided many places of refuge and led me to people and places that would understand my journey and were able to provide me with the information I so desperately needed. I call it a journey because I believe that life is a process of discovering our own true selves without limitations. I also believe that God has a perfect plan for all lives, and although we get bumps and bruises on the way, as long as we don't give up or cave in, we will not only discover some amazing truths about ourselves. We will also come to find that we have a God-given right to live a prosperous life here on earth. Navigating through the dark times of my life was tough. It hurt like hell as I experienced many days of hopelessness. I felt powerless because I didn't know how to cope with the trauma I had endured. Therefore, I believed every distorted thought and feeling that came to me as result of my sexual abuse. Self-obsession coupled with fear shaped my life, and drugs became the solution to what seemed to be a mental and emotional dilemma. My false sense of courage and pride would lead me to jails and institutions as I experienced a spiritual death, and although it took a long time, energy, and a lot of therapy to find my voice, it was well worth it.

If you are reading this book while serving a life sentence in prison for a drug-related crime or sitting on the side of your bed contemplating suicide because death seems much easier than living, or maybe you haven't been living at all—just existing with a bagful of feelings and emotions that seemingly control every decision you make, searching for that someone or something to make your mess of a life better—or just different. Before you resort to drastic measures, please hold on for a little while longer. I would like to offer up a suggestion.

Take a moment to escape your thoughts by not listening to what your mind may be telling you about you! Listen only to your breath. Whatever it may be doing, connect yourself there. As you connect to your breath, close your eyes, breathing deeply, exhaling slowly and completely! Make your request known to the God of your understanding by whatever voice you have; yell, scream, cry, or just say a silent prayer! Not to your parents' God or your grandparents' God but the one that connects to your spirit, then take a couple of more deep breaths, inhaling so deeply until your lungs expand fully, and then exhale every part of your breath until you feel the trauma escape out of your lungs, then open your eyes and surrender to a power greater than any other power by removing yourself out of your own way while allowing the God of your understanding to work on your behalf.

While many books have been written about abuse, the intent of this story is to share a journey of recovery and to send a message of hope to addicts and to victims of abuse that we do recover.

Abuse has many facets—physical, verbal mistreatment, assault, violation, and rape—and does not discriminate based on race, gender, age, religion, or sexual orientation.

ACTIVE ADDICTION

God, grant me knowledge that I may write in your divine precepts and instill in me a sense of your purpose.

I lived with the horrors of active addiction for more than twenty years, feeling trapped, shameful, and unworthy, while fighting every day to try and hold it together. What I know now that I didn't know then was that the fight was spiritual and much bigger than I could ever be in my humanness; therefore, I was broken, and my own worst enemy was me! I made terrible choices and put myself in situations that should have killed me. Fear, anger, and resentment controlled my life and gave birth to many other defects that kept me confused and on a mission to destroy everything good in my life. These character defects lived so deep down in my soul and would often scream so loudly that if I had the courage, I would have taken my own life long before now. I really just wanted the pain to stop and the noise between my two ears to go away, which no one else could hear except me, and I didn't know how to shut up the voices that would tell me that I was guilty of the secrets that kept me sick, and if I exposed them, in some way my entire family would be destroyed. I didn't know that I could do anything about my pain except to feel it, so I suffered in silence, and for many years I lived with the guilt, the shame, and embarrassment of my victimization. I had very little coping skills and no self-love. I hated myself and the world around me. I blamed every man for the abuse I had endured! I blamed my father for not being there to protect me! I blamed my mother for not hearing my silent cry out for help! I blamed God for not being almighty in my world, and for everything else I blamed myself! My own self-inflicted abuse turned out to be much worse than anything that anyone else had done to me because I wanted so desperately to change the way I felt and I thought my only option was to sell my soul to a very dark and destructive path called addiction.

I was able to hold it together for periods at a time by not using and seemingly fixing myself by my outward image, using my set of intellectual skills to convince everyone that I was well, but eventually I would return to my vomit over and over again with no explanation to why. I even stayed clean long enough to give birth to a healthy, beautiful baby girl, but it wasn't long before my family had to intervene because I was to self-centered and in a state of deep denial that I had convinced myself that I could handle my own life. When my momma would question my parenting capabilities, I would often respond with an arrogant tone, saying, "I love my baby, and I would never allow anything bad to happen to her, so don't you worry about it!" God knows I loved my baby with everything in me; unfortunately, there wasn't much in me operating from a place of love! The real story was that I was an addict from the pit of my soul, addicted to fear, anger, resentments, and drugs, and I desperately needed a solution. I was like a train headed the wrong way on the tracks, not realizing that I would eventually crash; nevertheless, nothing was more important than getting my "feel good," and that was my painful reality.

> *God, grant me the ability to be honest, open, and transparent. Help me to stay focused and fearless. Amen.*

MY STORY

I was born in Chattanooga, Tennessee, in the early sixties when children were just children—nothing more and nothing less. I grew up fatherless, like many black children, and had only seen a picture of a man in a military suit—a very tall, slender, and handsome man—and was told that he was Dad. In spite of my missing dad, Mom came through, like most black mommas would, with a stepdad named Rich. I didn't know much about him except that he seemed really angry most of the time. While only observing from afar, I would notice his discontentment. I wanted a dad, but this was not him, and I knew that he was not to be trusted, so at an early age, I learned how to put on that fake smile and hide my feelings when my stepdad was around and how to pretend that everything was good.

My stepdad brought along three kids of his own—a beautiful, light-skinned, tall girl with long hair and two boys. I also remember two other grown men being in our home on a regular, which were my stepdad's brothers, and it's still unclear if the brothers lived with our family or were regular visitors. I had four biological siblings, which consisted of two sisters and two brothers, so at one time, there were eight kids in the home, and although there was a lot of good times in the home among the siblings, what I remembered the most was the anger, the fear, a lot of beatings, and a lot of crying; so I tried to be a good girl, like Grandma would remind me on our summer visit, saying, "Be a good girl now, and I'll see you later," but I was a sneaky kid, so unfortunately I always managed to get my share of beatings. Although I resided in a large family, I felt different, like I didn't belong in my family, and I would soon be going home to my real family, and although there was never a real destination, I could imagine a family full of love and no fear, where I would feel safe and a part of. I was a finger sucker and a chunky kid, and when I was afraid, food and my finger would bring me comfort.

I loved my sister Bria. She was a couple of years older than me, and the one that took care of me most of the time, so I would stay close to her a lot, but Bria had a lot of responsibility taking care of the smaller kids, and sometimes it was apparent that she wasn't thrilled with my neediness, oftentimes pushing me away with anger; and although I knew that she loved me, I would feel rejected and unworthy. As a small child, I didn't understand that Bria was just a child herself and not equipped to handle my insecurities. Bria was a beautiful girl, and it was widely known that she was the prettier of us two as she was praised when other family members would visit. They would immediately notice her beauty and poise. Bria was also my momma's little helper, and I was nobody but a scared little girl. Fat momma was my name, and everybody knew it. Even relatives when they would visit called me fat momma as they would rave about my sister Bria. My thoughts would sometimes be magnified, and I would talk to myself with questions like "Why couldn't I be pretty and adored?" or "Why am I the helpless one, always needing someone to hold my hand and help me?" I was even afraid to go to the bathroom alone at night, so I would often wake up Bria in tears.

I didn't believe that anyone in the family really liked me. Instead, I believed that they laughed at me in secret. "Take that finger out your mouth" was what I heard over and over again, so I learned to hide in shame. "Give me a hug," the uncles would say when they would visit, and I hated them touching me about as much as I hated my body. I cried in silence so much that as a child I learned how not to cry at all. Even when I got my beatings, I refused to cry, and although I had so much to say, I never felt important enough to say it. Sometimes I wanted to scream for help, but I just didn't know what I needed help for, so oftentimes I would talk to myself and make pretend that I was someone and somewhere else.

Maybe I was born with self-obsession. As a matter of fact, I think all children are, but mine was very extreme. There were times when I would hold on to a feeling and would not let it go for days on end, lurking around the house, listening to and looking at everything, as my curiosity would definitely get the best of me because in those days kids didn't have a say so as to what went on in the home. In no way were we allowed to share our thoughts or ask questions about anything of importance. Instead, we did what we were told, and that was it, so after many slaps in the mouth for speaking my opinion, I learned to shut my mouth and keep all thoughts and feelings to myself, and when I did find the courage to speak out, it usually didn't turn out well, at least not for me.

THE GREEN HOUSE

Some of my earliest childhood memories are from a street called Greenwood Road in Chattanooga, Tennessee. It was a big green house with a wooden swing set in the backyard. Vaguely I can remember a chicken coop behind the house and my momma bringing in fresh chickens to cook for dinner. I could also hear Rich, my stepdad, yelling, "Don't y'alls get on this swing set. I ain't done with it yet!" I must have been a little rebellious at an early age because the memory of that same swing set crashing down on my head would hunt me years later!

I shared a large room with my three sisters, where we slept in a set of bunk beds, and in the middle of the night, I could see a man's shadow as he would creep into our room. I was usually holding myself afraid to go to the bathroom and trying not to wet the bed, oftentimes unsuccessfully because some nights Bria wouldn't wake up to go to the bathroom with me, and I was too afraid to go alone. Terrified with my head half-covered when suddenly one of my sisters would scream as the man would run out of the room. Rich would come running in with his robe on and his gun in hand, then he would run around the house checking to see if the intruder was still there. Out the front door Rich would go, and he would have definitely shot the man that was in the girls' room if he had caught him, but the intruder would get away every time.

"*Go back to sleep*," Momma would say in a shaky, still sleepy voice. "*There's no one here. The house is locked up!*"

At the time I was too young to think or even question why didn't the police ever come, and I could never understand how Rich and Momma didn't know who this man was creeping through the house because it happened so often that we eventually gave the creeper a name, calling him the tennis-shoe man.

I knew who the man was that was coming into the girls' room at night, but I couldn't tell anyone because during the day this same man would take me into a room and lay on top of me, humping on me and feeling on by body. He called it a game, telling me that it was a secret game. "This is our secret. Don't tell anyone," the man would say! Only about six or seven years old at the time, my small brain couldn't comprehend what was happening, but I did know that it was a bad thing because it felt weird. But I trusted him because he was a grown-up, and I had been taught to do what the grown-ups told me to do, so I believed him when he said that if Momma found out, she would be really mad at me, and I would get a beating, so I did as the man said and kept that secret to myself. I was being trained early on how to keep secrets and how to babysit my fear and besides all the kids often got into trouble over something, and a beating was usually the outcome, and since beatings could come from any adult family member, I was reluctant to say anything to anybody—about an adult anyway.

HE CREEPS

He creeps through the day and creeps through the night. My mind never rests! Is this a test or trial? How many more do I have in this place? My space is so crowded. Thoughts, plots, and plans of others all bundled up inside my mind while he creeps, "I can't sleep." I watch mysteriously as he roams like a lion, destroying all that he can! When the sun has gone down and the moon is at bay, he creeps—feeling, touching, smiling, running, dreading the morning as it brings the memories of the night as he wonders around curiously, invasively, then he's gone like a ghost! He moves fast, can't catch up, gone with the wind, like Dorothy down the yellow brick road, as he creeps.

My stepbrothers, Lonnie or Junior, would oftentimes fall down on the floor or on the ground outside, where us kids played, as I could hear Momma yell, "Get me a spoon!" Sherri or Bria would respond like military soldiers on command, running and returning with a spoon. They were the older sisters and always knew what to do. It only took one yell from Momma, and they were there, but me, I would run to see if the stepbrother was dead this time as my mom would shove the spoon into his mouth, shouting, "Stand back, I need some room!" I would tremble and watch his eyes roll around in his head until it was over. Afterward, we would continue on with the day going on quietly as though nothing had happened—no explanation! Unlike the family on the television show *Leave It to Beaver* or

The Waltons, when an incident happened, there were no family discussions or hugs, no wiping tears away to reassure us kids that everything would be fine! What I didn't know then is that my stepbrothers were having what is known as epileptic seizures, and being untreated would eventually have an impact on their futures.

THE JOURNEY CONTINUES

In the midsixties, my family moved to Detroit, Michigan, where my momma and stepdad both got jobs at the automobile plants. Detroit was known as the *Motor City*, where minorities could make a decent living working in the car industry. Detroit is also known as the home of Motown Records, founded by the one and only Berry Gordy Jr., where many old-school musical icons were created out of Motown, like Michael Jackson, Diana Ross, the Temptations, Marvin Gaye, Stevie Wonder, Smokey Robinson, and none other than *the Queen of Soul*, Aretha Franklin. Detroit was a family city with many opportunities and lots of history. I've often thought about returning to "my city" to live, but the memories and all the hell I experienced in active addiction would leave me sick to my stomach.

Our first home in Detroit was a huge three-story home on a street called Trowbridge. It was beautiful and eerie all at the same time, and I was always scared! A strange lady would come and stand on the porch, demanding that we leave what she called her house. She was a very large and scary lady and would come by mostly when Momma and Rich were not home; standing on the front porch, she would be looking into the window, yelling, "Get out of my house!" Us kids would run screaming and hiding until she would eventually leave. The house reminded me of one from a scary movie, and I'm not sure where the story came from that the scary lady's husband might have died in our house, and that she was coming back to take back her property was true or not, but coupled with my own fear, it was terrifying.

It was common for my stepdad to get upset at the dinner table for any reason as I was never sure why he would yell at Lonnie or

Junior or sometimes both and, *wham*, knock them onto the floor and summon one or both of them to the basement to what I called the beating room. I was terrified at just the thought of that basement! I was afraid that someday I would have to go there and get a beating myself by Rich. As the dinner dishes were finished, Momma would make her command as usual, "Sherri, make sure everyone gets their bath, and get Bria to help you put those kids' pajamas on," as she would march up the stairs and go into a room that seemed dark and mysterious, a room that always terrified me, a room that I considered the dungeon, her bedroom.

I would tremble as the door would shut as I looked from afar, screaming inside loudly, as I would not dare say a word. My thoughts would race across my mind, like a train rolling down the tracks to the next stop and then the next. I couldn't help wondering what kind of horrible things went on in that room. I never heard any laughter coming from that room, only cries. The door was always shut, and Rich would usually shy away right after dinner to that dungeon of a room and wouldn't come out until the next day. I would imagine some hero like Superman coming to rescue Momma, busting the door down, bringing her out, and flying away with her and us kids never again to return, and I swore to myself that I would never let any man lock me up in a room or beat on me or my kids.

My earliest memory of school in Detroit was around fourth grade, and the only feeling I recall is fear. I can remember having what seemed to be an out-of-body experience while sitting in class watching the other kids laughing and talking, thinking about my secrets and feeling guilty, ashamed and afraid that the other kids would know if I didn't keep my composure. I wanted to like school and be like the other kids with friends, but I felt different. I wanted to stay home so that I could watch my mom, and although I was just a child, I felt as though I could protect her in some way by just being there and watching. I was always afraid in or out of the house, and I couldn't find a reason to laugh, and I was afraid to make friends because I thought if anyone really knew who I was and the horrible things I had done, they would not want to be my friend anyway, and I would be judged, ridiculed, and laughed at.

JUST A CHILD

I try to hold my head up high as I cry inside. I'm in this place, where others reside, I pretend to be a part of with my cute ponytails and fake smile. No one knows that my legs are trembling underneath the wooden desk. I'm just a child with grown-up experiences, filled with insecurities that I refuse to share. My heart beats fast as I notice the stares. Please don't like me or try to entice me. I'm a bad girl! You don't know my secrets, and I'm not telling anyone—ever. I suck my finger and hold my pillow tight at night, trembling, shaking in fear of the unknown, so don't beg for my attention by looking my way. You don't know my secrets, and I'm not telling anyone—ever.

I often dreamed of becoming a singer and a dancer. It was what I loved to do. I watched a lot of television as a child, and one of my favorite shows was the Shirley Temple show. She was a child dancer and singer, and I felt most happy when I was watching her sing and dance. I was often in school plays during my elementary school days, and I can remember my momma coming to see me perform. I would be holding my breath until I would look out in the audience and see her because oftentimes I had an overwhelming feeling of fear that she would find out my secret and be mad and not come, and as horrible as it sounds, I would even think that Rich would do something bad to her, and she might be dead and couldn't come.

I didn't want others to know that at home we were not happy. No one was happy, not my sisters, my brothers, or me. At least, that was my perception, and my momma was just a figment of my imagination because I didn't feel close to her at all. She was so beautiful, and I wanted to touch her every day, but she seemed to be out of reach and out of touch with my emotional state of being, so I would just watch her and wish that I could say the words that my childlike mind was thinking, such as, *"Come hug me! I'm afraid! I don't know what to do or how to feel or why I feel the way I do!"* I needed her, not my sisters because they were not equipped to deal with my hurt and trauma, but maybe momma wasn't either.

I believe my mom gave us kids all she had to give, and maybe she didn't realize that parenting was much more than she could provide five children—or eight for that matter—and she took on too much responsibility. Maybe momma didn't know I was afraid and if I could have only been a big girl and told her, but I couldn't! Maybe she did know and was just in deep denial herself because the pain of dealing with it could have been too much for her to handle, and the only way to cope was for her to look the other way. There were so many maybes that I didn't know where to begin to answer them or address them alone, so instead I began stuffing them, and I became numb inside, and sometimes I would become overwhelmed by my feelings and emotions, but I kept quiet.

THE ESCAPE

I was asleep in my bed when I was frantically awakened: *"Get up! Put these clothes on! Hurry up!"* It was my sister Bria in a soft but stern voice, saying, *"Come on, get up, hurry!"*

Rubbing the sleep out of my eyes, dizzy but following instructions like I always did, my eyes must have looked like I was running from a bear chasing me in the woods. *Up I jumped.* "*Where we going?*" I asked.

"Just come on, girl!" Bria replied. I followed my sister down the steps of the spooky house, not sure what to think while she was shoving bags in my hand. *"Carry this to the car and hurry!"* I was half awake and moving as fast as I could, looking around with curious eyes at the same time.

Again and again I continued to ask, "*Where we going?*" but I was getting no answer, just a command from Bria: *"Just hurry up, girl, and get down those stairs!"*

After we loaded up the car with our bags and us five kids, my momma jumped in the driver's seat and began backing out of the driveway, still no answers as where we were going. I began to think maybe we were leaving this haunted house for good, but as I glanced out of the back window as the car was driving away, I could see my stepsister Sherri standing there, her body getting smaller and smaller as the car drove farther and farther away. I began to wonder why we were leaving her and where Lonnie and Junior were, but I was afraid to ask another question, knowing there would be no answers, leaving me unsure what to think about this ride off into the night—to where? I had so many different thoughts, and feelings were going on inside of me, but I was too young to identify any of them or to express how I must have felt at the time, so I put my finger into my mouth and laid my head on Bria's shoulder, comforting myself as we rode off to an unknown place. What I didn't realize then that I realized today is that this experience taught me how to run, and I've been running ever since!

We moved to an apartment building directly across the street from what looked like a big old abandoned school building, and I would soon find out that it was my future school. When I think back, we had some rough times in that apartment. I can recall either not having a refrigerator at all or having one that was not working because I have visions of Momma hanging food out the window in plastic bags in the winter time. I was a sleepwalker, and I would sometimes urinate in the towel closet or wander outside at night, so I can only imagine what my momma had to endure to take care of us kids on her own and not to mention the jobs that she had work to keep food on the table. School had always been and still was a struggle for me. A new school and a new home should have been a new opportunity, but my secrets always followed me, and this rough school was not helping. The yelling in the hallways was a definite sign of chaos, and there was never a dull moment in class, and the girls were always fighting, and the boys would sit on the steps as the girls would walk up and down so that they could look under our skirts. I was afraid to even try to make friends—and wasn't sure that I even wanted to.

I met two girls that were twins and very pretty, but I don't remember their names. What I do remember is that they were good girls—Campfire Girls—and I wanted to be like them, so I begged my momma to let me join Campfire Girls, and she did. My first trip to the theater was with my new friends and their mom, and when I saw the opera, it was the most amazing thing I had ever seen! I was totally in love with the voices of the opera singers and could imagine myself on stage singing right along with them. The twins were happy, and I could see it as they sat beside me in the opera, smiling in their cute ponytails and identical flower-print dresses, and they both had their legs crossed like Grandma used to cross hers when she would sit on the front porch. I knew that the twins didn't have any secrets, and I could tell that no one had ever touched them in places that made them feel weird, so I didn't feel like I could ever measure up to them, but I tried to at least look perfect just like them, so I crossed my legs too.

Every day brought new challenges at my new school, and on many of those days, I would run home to keep from fighting. I didn't know how to fight; in fact, I don't think I had ever had a fight. We came from a big beautiful house, and even though it was a bit scary, it was quiet in the neighborhood, and the school I came from, there was never any fighting. The teachers cursed and hit the kids like they were grown-ups, and this was so different from what I had ever seen. At least the abuse that I was used to was not out in the open, and only family members were allowed to abuse you. But now this was the real world, and I could see that abuse was acceptable everywhere. I had to learn how to deal with it. For a while it was tough, but I tried to go to school and do the right thing, but as time went on, it got harder to have friends because I didn't fit in with the good girls or the bad girls.

I was still in drama classes, and I still loved performing on stage because I just felt free of fear even if it was just for a while. I could feel good about myself. My momma had to work more, and I had to walk home usually with my little brother Cedi, and although the school was across the street from where we lived, some days it felt like the longest walk in the world. I sometimes had to run home for just looking at a girl or a boy because I didn't want to talk to them. One day my sister caught me running home and told my mom like she told everything else! Momma said to me, *"If you run home again, I will beat you all the way back to school. You better fight back!"* I didn't want to fight, and I didn't even know how to fight. No one had taught me how to fight, so I wanted to ask Momma what I was supposed to do in a fight, but as usual I didn't say anything except "Yes, ma'am."

It was a living hell at this school, and my hate for school was growing deeper and deeper every day. My choices were to either fight or run and then get beat by momma, so I began to fight, and I never stopped. Not only did I start fighting back, but I also started cussing back at the teacher, skipping school, and stealing candy at the local grocery store. One thing led to another, and I lost all control and became totally defiant. My momma didn't like the fact that I was getting out of control, but she had told me to fight back, and that's what I was doing. I started to get expelled from school, and this was just the beginning. I began to hang out with the bad girls, and my friendship with the twins drifted away. For the first time I had some friends who liked me, and we could laugh and do exciting things together even though they were not the better choice. I was still afraid of the kids at school, but I knew how to fight now, and I had some bad girlfriends, so I didn't have to worry so much anymore.

Lana was my momma's friend from down the street. She was a single mom as well, and she and mom would sometimes go out in the evenings together. Lana had three children of her own—Roxie, Venus, and Danny—and we would sometimes stay together in the evenings when Momma and Lana would go out on the town. Danny was the oldest, and he was in special education class. I remember that because his class was in the basement at the school, and that's where the special ed kids went to class. He was so mean to his sisters and would beat them up almost every time we were left alone with them, and even though he was special in his learning abilities, he was very cute, and he liked me, and there were times when he would protect me from the boys at school. One time as I was running home after school because a boy was following me. I didn't understand boys. They were just weird, and if they liked a girl, they would pick on you and chase you around. I just didn't like them at all. One certain boy had been trying to talk to me and would often wait for me after my drama class, which was held after school, and I would run home because I was afraid of him. One day after drama class there he was, waiting for me. Off I ran right into Danny. He asked if I was okay, and I told him that this same boy followed me every day. Off he ran to catch up with the boy, and he beat that boy something terrible, and I never had a problem again with boys.

Early one summer morning, my Auntie Eva, Momma's baby sister, came to visit. I remember hearing Momma crying and talking to my auntie, and soon after, us kids were packed up and moved to

Chattanooga, leaving my mom behind. To this day I still don't know what happened and why we left her! See, we didn't have the privilege of asking questions and getting answers as kids do today. We just did what we were told to do and kept our mouths shut, or somebody would shut it for you! It didn't matter who as long as they were a family member and your elder. I'm not sure how long we were there in Chattanooga, but when we returned, we had a new house on the west side of Detroit on a street called Littlefield, and it was much nicer than the apartment on the east side of the city. The neighbors even looked different. It was quiet and clean, and the kids seemed to be a lot nicer than the ones on the east side of town.

That year, we were introduced to a new fight called racism as we were bused to a predominately white school, riding every day on a yellow school bus, which would pick us up and take my sister and I to Rudman Junior High. Our school bus was a target most days on the ride home because the white kids would throw rocks at our school bus, often breaking the windows and sometimes injuring one of the black kids, which would usually result in fights the next day. This went on for probably a year, but eventually the feud was over between the white and black kids, and we started to fight one another again for whatever reason.

We couldn't wait to get outside after we got home from school. We loved to play outside especially softball, which we would meet up in the streets with the kids in the neighborhood or play on the railroad tracks jumping in and out of the parked trains until the streetlights came on. You didn't let the streetlights catch you outside! You better be on that porch when those streetlights came on, or you had to deal with Momma, and that was not nice!

HAPPY TIMES

We usually spent our summer months with Grandma Hat in Chattanooga, which I loved because I loved my grandma so much. She worked as a maid, and she would sometimes take me to work with her on the bus. The bus ride was when the maids talked about their bosses that they worked for and how ridiculous their job duties were. But not Grandma. She loved all her bosses, and she didn't take no mess off any of them; in fact, she would tell them what she was going to do and what she was not going to do, and they loved and respected her, saying, *"Okay, Hat, just do what you gon' do!"*

Grandma would always buy me a big peppermint and give me $5 on the way home. She would say, *"I'm going to 'vide with you what I made today."* My grandma was the cutest little lady with her pigeon toes, and she could walk for miles and not get tired and talk at the same time, and if she saw anybody's kids in mischief, she would stop and put her hand on her hip and chastise them, and they would just say, *"Yes, ma'am, Ms. Hat."* They knew Grandma didn't take any mess and that she knew their parents because she knew everybody, and they loved and respected her.

As we got off the bus to walk home, one of her neighbors would speak to her, saying, *"Hey, Ms. Hat, who you got there?"*

She would introduce me to everybody, saying, *"This is my granddaughter from Detroit. They visiting me."* Grandma would respond with her hand on her small hip, wearing her curly black wig. *"I'm comin' from work, and I got to go cook dinner. I'll talk wit' cha later!"* My grandma could cook anything without a recipe or a box. She would just put in a pinch of this and a pinch of that, and we would have the best meal ever, and her hot-water corn bread and fried peach pies were the best in the world.

Grandma was the lady in the neighborhood that knew no stranger, and she fed everybody, and you better not have any dirty kids because they would definitely get a bath if they came to Grandma's house. She was also an entrepreneur, selling frozen icies and cold Coca-Colas in the summer, and she kept her money in a big jar. I would watch her count her money as she rolled her coins, saying, *"We made a good penny today!"* Grandma never did remarry, and she seemed to be content with her life and didn't seem to need much except her family, and she was good if we were good. I once asked her if she would get married again, and she replied, *"The Bible says that a man only gets one wife, so I will always be your granddad's wife."* Although my grandfather was on his second wife at the time and would soon remarry for the third time, Grandma still thought of herself as his only wife. When I think about how simple her life was and the fact that she didn't need much to be happy, she was my hero, and although Grandma didn't have much, she was still always willing to give to others.

My grandma was a strong and humbled woman, but at the same time she didn't take crap from anybody. Grandma would say things to us, like, *"Don't argue about it. Let the Lord have it. He can do a better job than you."* I can remember Grandma singing the songs "Jesus Loves Me" and "When We All Get to Heaven." And although she told us not to argue, she also reminded us to always fight back and not allow anyone to treat us bad. She would say, *"My daddy told me to always fight back!"* One of grandma's sayings that I still live by today is, *"Never trust a liar! If they lie, they will cheat. If they cheat, they will steal. And if they steal, they will kill."* Although in active addiction, I lied a lot especially when I was afraid for my life, and there were many of those times. But I honor my grandmother today by being honest to the best of my ability with myself and others, and besides, lying takes too much energy.

My grandma loved her daddy. He was her hero till the day she died. She talked about him as if he was the only man in her life, and her face would light up with a smile as she would stand up and put her hand on her small hip, saying, *"When I was a child, my daddy didn't let nobody bother me, not even my momma!"* As she continued to rave about her father, she would also say, *"I was my daddy's baby!"* She told us many stories about how he never worked for anybody because he had his own farm and how all her siblings worked on the land they owned except her because she was the baby and her dad's favorite child. She loved to go to church and read the Bible, and I think my grandma recited her favorite scripture, the Twenty-third Psalm, at least once a day every day:

> *The Lord is my shepherd; I shall not want. He maketh me to lie down in green pastures: he leadeth me beside the still waters. He restoreth my soul: he leadeth me in the paths of righteousness for his name's sake. Yea, though I walk through the valley of the shadow of death, I will fear no evil: for thou art with me; thy rod and thy staff they comfort me. Thou preparest a table before me in the presence of mine enemies: thou anointest my head with oil; my cup runneth over. Surely goodness and mercy shall follow me all the days of my life: and I will dwell in the house of the Lord forever.*

My grandma gave us a lot of words of wisdom to live by, and I heard her, but I just didn't know how to listen to her. She was my grandma. She was not supposed to tell me how to live. She was just supposed to love me and give me $5 and a peppermint, but I didn't know what I know now, and I took from her what I wanted and not what I needed. I even stole Grandma's money in active addiction, but still when I got out of jail with nowhere to go, after being locked up for almost two weeks for fighting in the street over drugs, she let me come stay with her with no hesitation. My grandma was the one person I knew for sure that loved me no matter what I did, but I used her, and I didn't give her my undivided attention. I didn't write down her recipes. Even though they were a pinch here and a pinch there, they still made sense and a good meal but only if I had just listened. No one told me how much knowledge grandmothers had! No one told me that someday I would regret not listening closely to her stories because they had meaning, and no one said that those small words that didn't seem to mean much at the time would come to mean a lot, and those intimate words coming from Grandma should have been tucked away for later. I had been clean for a few years when my grandma went to heaven, so I got a chance to hold her in my arms and make amends to her for all the hurt and pain I caused her and tell her how much I loved and appreciated her for all her unconditional love—and her fried peach pies.

Our summers in Chattanooga visiting my cousins were especially fun. Lea was my age, and Trina, who was always on Lea's little hip, was the second oldest. Lea carried Trina around like she was a baby doll. It was the cutest thing ever, and I loved Lea. She was so pretty with dark skin and long black hair and very thin, and I could tell that my auntie adored her as well. I wanted to be like her because she was so smart, and she could fight too. Lea always got what I wanted for Christmas and would show it off to me when I would visit, especially when she got the Easy-Bake Oven, and I was so jealous because Momma couldn't afford it, so when I would visit Lea for the summer, I cooked on Lea's Easy-Bake Oven, and she let me, but I was still jealous.

My auntie was pretty too, and I loved her so much because she was so nice to us and always treated us like her kids when we would visit for the summer. She also had three other kids—Fefe, Erin, and Junior—and their father, Riley, was my auntie's third husband. He seemed nice at first, but I was afraid of him, and I really didn't know why. I noticed that my grandma didn't care for him, and he didn't care much for her either. I always had a weird kind of feeling around him, but I was scared of all men, and when he would fuss at my auntie at the dinner table, it reminded me of my stepdad, Rich, how he would make a fuss at the boys over dinner for whatever reason, so again I wore a fake smile every time I was around my auntie's husband and pretended to be okay.

My auntie and her husband attended the Church of God in Christ, where they had some strict rules and would only allow females to wear long dresses and no pants. I didn't know much about religion except when Grandma would pray her prayer and tell us kids to pray along with her and when auntie would have us say our prayers at night, and there was also a time when Momma would order these prayer cloths and religious candles, and she watched a religious man on television, and I could hear him saying, "*You can't lose with the stuff I use!*" That summer, my auntie took us to her church, and we wore long dresses just like she and Lea did, but when we returned home, Momma was not happy about it, so we went back to wearing our blue jeans.

BREAKING POINT

The summer of 1974, I turned twelve years old, and I can remember like it was yesterday. My brother Cedi and I would usually have our birthday parties together since we both were born in May, and I had gotten new summer clothes for my birthday because my mom had said that I was getting too big for my old clothes. I already had acquired the name fat momma, and I hated it, but it was what the grown folks called me, so I didn't make a fuss about it other than a frown on my face every now and then. I was a chunky kid and loved to eat sweets, especially Grandma's fried peach pies and Momma's homemade chocolate chip cookies, and sometimes in the night, I would sneak cookies on my way to the bathroom. I remember arguing with Momma that summer about going to Chattanooga because I didn't want to go, and I told her that I was not going back! She threatened me in anger, saying, *"Girl, if you say one more thing, I will slap you dead in your mouth!"*

I had several girlfriends by this time, so I wanted to stay home, dress up, and walk to the store and around the neighborhood with them and talk about boys and what girl we had a fight with or who we wanted to fight. That's what we did when the weather was nice. We would also still play softball from time to time, and I loved riding my bike with my brother Cedi on the handle bars even though we would usually crash, but after he would stop crying, we would do it all over again. The neighborhood kids would sometimes fight after the softball games for some ungodly reason, but we would meet the next day on the same corner to do it all over again until the streetlights came on, then hightail it home. I tried my best to convince Momma to let me stay home that summer, but like every other debate I had lost, I would lose this one as well, and a few days after school let out, off to Chattanooga we went.

This summer was different because Bria didn't have to go to Chattanooga, just me and the smaller kids, and I was fire-hot mad because Bria always got her way! She was the oldest and the prettiest, and Momma seemed to like her best, and of course, she helped Momma out more than I did, so I guess there was just no chance of me staying home for the summer. Usually, once I got to Chattanooga, it was fine because I always liked hanging out with my cousin Lea. She was my favorite cousin and my best friend. So once I got over being mad at my mom for not letting me stay home, I was okay.

It was an early morning, and I was at my auntie's house asleep when I was awakened with a nudge. *"Wake up,"* he said, *"and come with me!"* I got up and was led to the bedroom where he and my auntie shared. A huge bed was what I saw as I wiped the sleep out of my eyes. I was confused as to what was happening as he began to tie something around my eyes, and I could feel his hands leading me forward. Gently setting me on the bed, he pushed me onto my back into a lying position. I felt my pajama pants being pulled down and a heavy force on top of me. Everything seemed to happen so fast that I couldn't take in all that was happening. Fear rushed through me as though I was being thrown down a flight of stairs as I lay there terrified, thinking what was happening as I realized I was experiencing my first ever sexual encounter with my uncle!

I had been touched in private places and humped on by the strange man whom we called the tennis-shoe man, but this was different! He was very gentle with me as he said, *"I won't hurt you, just relax."* Before I could process any of his, I was being led blindfolded to another room, and as the blindfold was being removed, I could hear a voice whisper in my ear, saying, *"Clean yourself up, and if you tell anybody about this, I will kill everybody in this house, but I love you!"* I was so afraid to open my eyes that I kept them shut until I heard the door close, then slowly my eyes opened, and I could see the bathroom sink, so I began to do as he instructed and wash myself. I remember looking in the mirror and not seeing the same reflection that I usually saw. This wasn't me. This was a twelve-year-old girl that had been left in the bathroom very confused with yet another secret.

I had done it again—allowed another man to touch me in a way that I knew Momma would not approve of. I did what I was told, but this time it didn't feel like a game. It was different. This time he said he loved me and that he would kill me at the same time, and I just couldn't wrap my twelve-year-old brain around what had just happened. Had I just been raped, or did this happen to all girls at this age? Besides, he did say that he did this to my sister and my cousin, so why didn't they tell somebody so I wouldn't have been left there with him? I couldn't ask any questions, and I couldn't tell Lea or my auntie when they came home because I didn't want them to die, so I knew I couldn't tell even if I wanted to. I can remember thinking, "Is this love? Is this what I have to look forward to in the future? The gentle touch of a man, waking me up out of my sleep, blindfolding me, doing whatever he pleases, and then threatening my life, following that up with 'But I love you.' Is this the part they don't show in the movies, the death threat?" I wanted to just run and scream, but there was nowhere to go! I wanted to cry, but to whom? No one was there!

I had all those feelings but nowhere to put them, so I began to just stuff them deep inside. I cried really hard in the bathroom that morning, and then I stopped, and I screamed really loud inside that morning, and then I stopped. Bria was not there to comfort me, so I had to comfort myself, and there was no Jesus that Grandma and my auntie talked about in that bathroom with me! Had He forgotten about me that day! I was convinced that He let the men do what they wanted to do, and that was it! I was tired of keeping secrets, but I knew I had to keep this one. Besides, I didn't even know what had just happened. How would I tell this, and how could I describe what had just happened to me?

I thought about running out of that apartment that morning, but I was too afraid. As I watched the tears rolling down that girl's face in the mirror that I didn't know, my heart was beating so fast that I could hardly catch my breath, and I began to cry uncontrollably, without a sound even coming out of my mouth. That morning in the bathroom, I decided that I wasn't going to pray anymore, and never would I go to church again, and if I had to go with my auntie, I would just pretend like everybody else. Besides, I really didn't think that God was real anyway. Maybe it's just a scare tactic to keep us kids in line, or maybe it's a black family thing. I was scared to come out of that bathroom, but I was also afraid to stay in there, so slowly opening the door, I returned to the room where the twin beds were, got into the bed, and covered my head and put my finger in my mouth, where I stayed until I heard my auntie's voice.

That summer pushed me to my breaking point, and I didn't even know what that meant. All I knew was that I was different and that I had one secret too many with nowhere to put it because I didn't have any more room in my secret compartment, but I couldn't dare tell anyone no matter how confused I was. I needed someone to hold my hand more than ever, but who could I turn to? My auntie had left me there with this man, and my momma was over seven hundred miles away, and my grandma was just my grandma. What could she do? Besides, I didn't want to be responsible for my family getting killed by this nice pedophile and possible murderer.

I was only twelve years old. Was I supposed to know what to do? Well, I didn't! I was embarrassed and, of course, afraid. No matter what other feelings I adopted, my fear was a part of my everyday life ever since I could remember. It wasn't just the fear of going to the bathroom. It wasn't the fact that I wasn't Momma's favorite child. It wasn't even my past secrets of playing that game with the tennis-shoe man and allowing him to hump on me that changed my life. It was something different this time. Not only had I been violated but my entire family's life had also been threatened all at one time, leaving me with so many feelings that I could not even begin to identify.

A NEW ATTITUDE

Returning home after that summer numb inside, I don't think I had the ability to feel anything anymore but fear. All I knew was that I hated my body, and I didn't want it anymore. Besides, it had been taken away from me, so it didn't belong to me anyway. As if these weren't enough trauma for the year, I went to the bathroom, and there it was—I had gotten my period, and I was terrified! What did this mean? No one had explained to me that this thing happened naturally and that it was to be expected around age twelve, and I had no idea what was happening, so I thought maybe I was pregnant, and maybe if I told someone, they would know what I did this summer, and this would confirm what everybody suspected about me all along, that I was worthless and bad, so I flushed my panties down the toilet and ran out of the bathroom.

Bria was always checking on me. I think she knew that I was always afraid, and she wanted to protect me in a big-sisterly way. I sometimes resented her because she would always report everything I did to Momma, and I didn't feel any connection with Momma, and in some ways I never trusted her, so I was definitely not going to tell her my secret. My mom was a provider. She wasn't a storybook reader at night, and it took me a long time to understand that she gave us kids what she had to give and that everything she did on a daily basis was for us. She worked hard to provide a living for us, and that's what her momma had done for her and her two sisters, so that's what she knew to do for us. There were times when I would watch her cook our dinner and then hurry on out of the house for her day at the automobile plant, and when she would return home, she would go straight to bed, and sometimes I could hear her crying out to God for help to relieve her pain from working so hard. My mom was the most beautiful lady I had ever seen, but I felt as though she was unreachable and was only there to make sure us kids did the right thing all the time.

"Ooh, I'm telling Momma!" Bria shouted as she saw my panties floating on top of the water in the toilet. I didn't know what to say or do—run, hide, or lie—so I replied with a lie, "They ain't my panties," but before I could get the words out of my mouth, Bria had ran off and came back to show me what to do next. That day I learned about my menstrual cycle, and I hated it! It was symbol of torment, and I was so afraid that I had been exposed and that now Bria knew the horrible thing I had done, leaving me feeling ashamed. I didn't realize that this was a normal part of a girl's life and that it was supposed to be celebrated or cried over. I didn't know how to feel about it, so over the years, it had always been an embarrassing experience for me. It was a symbol of violation and shame, a hidden secret that I would continue to hide for many years to come.

I was so tired of keeping secrets, but I didn't know what to do with them because I was too young to compartmentalize any of my feelings. I just knew that I was a different person, and I knew I couldn't tell anybody what had happened to me that summer, or we could all die, so I tried to forget about it, but I couldn't forget. In fact, I would not be able to ever forget because the trauma had become a part of me, so no matter what I did or where I was, it was on my mind. I couldn't focus in school anymore, and I felt dirty, like I had been raped in the street behind a dumpster, and I was afraid for my family's life. Why didn't he just kill me so I wouldn't be afraid for my family every day? And every time I thought about it, I felt afraid again and wanted to cry, but I couldn't cry because I had cried my last cry in that bathroom, and I didn't have any more tears, so I pretended that I was okay. I couldn't sleep through the night anymore because I was afraid I would be awakened again by a strange man, and I couldn't get that image out of my head no matter what I did.

I started drinking alcohol and hanging out with the bad girls that lived down the block and lying to Momma like never before, and besides, she didn't know anything about my new friends. I could go to those girls' house anytime and drink because their mom didn't care. One day I asked Mom if I could go shopping with them and their momma, but since I was already on punishment, she was reluctant to allow me to go anywhere, but she gave me grace, saying, "You better be home before those streetlights come on!" but we had no plans to go shopping. Instead, we had other plans to meet up with some guys on the east side of town. It was way past curfew when I realized the time, and because this was all new to me, I thought I better call home, so I used the pay phone on the corner to let Mom know that I was on my way home. She was furious, shouting, *"Where are you?"* I told her where I was and that I was waiting for the bus. She replied, *"Keep your ass right there. I'm on my way!"* I was just praying for that bus to show up! I don't know how she got there so quickly, but in what seemed like only a few minutes, she pulled up in her black sedan, jumped out of that car, beat me in front of everybody, and threw me in the back of the car. Monday, it was all over school about how I got beat at the bus stop by my momma, and I was so embarrassed that I told everybody that she was my crazy aunt.

Jim was Momma's new boyfriend and had swindled his way into our home over the summer, and I did not like him at all because he was a bald-headed arrogant prick and talked all the time. Every time Momma fussed at us kids, he had something to say as if he had known us all our lives, and when he was drinking, he would take my two brothers for a ride, which I never could understand why Momma would let a drunken fool take her boys anywhere. Jim and Momma would fight a lot when he got drunk, and I was terrified that something bad would happen, and when we would call the police, they would say it was a family matter, and they could not intervene. I guess Momma had enough with Rich, my stepdad, beating her up, so she would fight Jim like a man, and afterward, he would either leave to cool off or they would just go to bed. I would think, *"What the hell is going on here!"* I wish Momma would just put this fool out and make him take all his clothes with him! I hated his guts especially when he would hang around the kitchen telling me how to wash the dishes. I would have visions of cutting his damn throat with a steak knife, and if he only knew how many times I thought of killing him in his sleep when he was drunk, he would have stayed far away from me. After all, I wouldn't tell anyone—I could keep secrets well!

Anette was my little sister, and she was adorable but meaner than a rattlesnake. I would have to braid her hair, and she hated it and would fight me the whole time, but Momma would make her sit there, and I loved braiding her hair because it made me feel important and like the big sister, but Anette, on the other hand, hated it and hated me for liking it. When she got in trouble and would get her beatings, she would run around the house, making Momma chase her, and I thought it was the funniest thing ever because I could tell that when Momma would catch her, she was completely out of breath, but when she did catch her, she would put my sister's head between her legs and beat her with a belt.

It was definitely different than it is now because nobody called the police or talked back to their parents, and when we got into trouble, a beating was the outcome. That was just the way it was. There was no discussing it or no time-out or no next time you do it because what Momma said was the rules, and Bria would make sure to report our bad behavior. My siblings would laugh at me when I got my beatings because I didn't cry, but I had learned to stuff my feelings instead of showing them, and besides, I didn't even know how to cry anymore. In fact, I didn't see any reason to cry because tears didn't do me any good. Instead, I believed that tears only meant that you were weak and bad, and even though I was both weak and bad, I wasn't going to show it.

FEELING MYSELF

I was maturing physically a great deal but mentally not so because my physical maturity for me meant more attention, and I did not want attention especially when Uncle Mac and Uncle Jeff would visit. They were huggers and would say to me, *"Give me a hug, girl!"* grabbing me and squeezing me tight as I would cringe in despair. They were Momma's favorite cousins, and she was always happy when they came to visit. I would just hold my breath until it was over and then run off to hide. I didn't want any man to touch me for any reason, and I was disgusted every time. I would hide in shame because I felt as though if I had not been so fat and needy, no one would have noticed me, and I tried to lose weight, but I didn't know how, so I lived in shame of my fat body every day.

I loved when Momma would bake homemade chocolate chip cookies on the weekend for us kids, so I would sneak into the kitchen when everyone was asleep and eat extra ones, and when she made her homemade cakes and let me lick the leftover mix out of the bowl, I felt close to her, and I felt that she needed me when she let me help her bake, so I would hang out in the kitchen to help her and to lick the bowl, but I wasn't really interested in learning how to cook. I was just in the kitchen to be next to my momma and for her to need me.

I remember coming home from school one day, and Jim was sitting on the couch holding a rifle. It all seemed to happen in slow motion as I walked past him. I heard a loud noise as the door frame in front of me shattered! Momma and Bria were huddled up in the bedroom, crying, and I didn't know what to do, so I felt like I had to protect them, and this was the first mad outbreak that I had ever had. As a sense of bravery came over me, I began to curse Jim like a mad black woman: *"You motherfucker!"* I yelled. *"I will kill you!"* I was tired of being afraid. This was it for me—no more fear of men! This fool almost killed me, and he's sitting there looking like a drunk zombie! I can remember the police coming to our house and taking Jim away, and soon afterward, he was gone for good. I decided that day that I hated all men and that they were all crazy, drunk, rapist pigs, and if you have them around, you better get them before they get you because either they are going to take over your house, violate your children, or kill you if you don't get rid of them first, and that was just the way it was.

During the summer of 1977, I didn't have to go to Chattanooga for the summer. Momma let me stay home, and I was happy about it. We had moved again, so there were no more softball games on the corner, and besides, I wasn't interested in softball anymore. I was almost fourteen years of age, and everything about me had completely changed except the fact that I hated school and men. Brooks Junior High was where I met Glenda. She was my ace boon coon, and we did everything together, even stole at the local Kmart. She wasn't a good girl or a bad girl. She was just Glenda, and I loved her. I had never stolen anything before I met Glenda except some Candy Dots at the supermarket once or twice, but Glenda was a pro, and she showed me how to put the clothes under my shirt neatly and walk out of the store.

Glenda was the oldest child of her siblings, and she called her momma by her name, Bay. Well, it wasn't her real name, but they were from Mississippi, and Glenda said everybody down South got nicknames, and Bay was her mama's, and her mom called her Lady, and I thought that was the cutest nickname for Glenda, so I wanted me a nickname, so I called myself Queen, and when I was with Glenda, that was my name, and I wasn't afraid of nothing. I was free from that scared little girl who had let people hug her and make her feel weird when she didn't want them to. No longer was I the timid one who allowed herself to be violated by uncles and humped on by people that pretended to care for her when all they really wanted was her body! I wasn't her when I was with Glenda! I was Queen, ready to steal, lie, skip school, and do whatever I wanted to, and nobody was going to stop me! Glenda wore makeup, and she liked boys, and she even smoked cigarettes, and I admired the bad girl in her. I had smoked marijuana a couple of times and had drunk wine coolers with my bad girlfriends and had even stayed out past curfew, but I always got caught by Momma, causing her to dislike my bad girlfriends. But Momma liked Glenda. She thought Glenda was nice and sweet, and she was nice and sweet, but Glenda could fool anybody, even Momma, and I was tickled pink.

Glenda had a little sister and a little brother that she kept after school until Bay got home from work, and she loved them both. She also had an uncle named Gene that came to visit often and was as fine as wine. He looked just like the singer Frankie Beverly, and I had a schoolgirl crush on him from the first time I saw him, and every time he would come over to Glenda's house, he would smile at me and say, *"Hello, Kiva,"* in a deep, sexy voice, so I just knew he secretly wanted me, but he didn't hug me like my uncles did, but I sure wanted him to, although if he had, I would have probably stopped crushing on him because I hated the thought of any man touching me.

Glenda and I went to Kmart often, and several times I didn't know that she was stealing until we left the store, and she would show me what she had underneath her clothes. She was that slick, and I was just in awe of how she could steal without me even knowing, but I was scared to steal anything in any store because I knew that I would get caught, like I always did when I tried to be bad, and Momma would kill me, so I got off on the fact that Glenda was such a pro. Glenda and I had the same birthday month, so on our fourteenth birthday, we decided that we would steal something from Kmart for our birthdays, and although I was scared to death, I decided after watching her steal for months that I was going to steal something and be as slick as she was, seeing as how she never got caught. I thought I could do it too, so I was ready.

When the security guard met me at the door, I was super scared, and at first I tried to act like I didn't know what he wanted until he said, "Follow me to the back room, ma'am." I was looking around for my friend but didn't see her anywhere until I was taken into the security office. To my surprise, there she was sitting at the table, looking like a career criminal with a stern look on her face. Glenda was giving me a side wink, like she was trying to tell me something, but I was so scared that I couldn't figure out what her wink meant. I just wanted to confess and go home, so I didn't have a clue as to what she was trying to say.

I was totally embarrassed as the police escorted us through the store in handcuffs while shoppers were looking and whispering. Talk about the longest walk ever. Glenda had given the security and the police officer a fake name and number, and she told me to do the same, so I did. As we sat in the jail waiting for the police to contact our parents with the wrong phone numbers, the sun was slowly going down. I could see it through the small window in the small room that we were sitting in. I couldn't help but wonder if I would spend the rest of my life in jail and that I was a criminal for the first time at age fourteen, at least a caught criminal, and I felt like my life was over!

That was the first time that I sat still and looked at *me* for just a while and wondered, What am I doing? Why did I do this? Neither of us wanted our parents contacted because we both knew that the hell was going to be beat out of us, so I waited as my friend planned our escape. "I'm going to break us out of here, so just be patient, and keep your mouth closed," said Glenda. I trusted her since she was such a pro at stealing, and I figured she must have a plan to get us out of this, so I did as she said and didn't say a word. I believe that my addiction was already a factor at that point in my life! I knew fear, shame, and guilt, but this was a new feeling called embarrassment that had entered my world. I began to think that maybe smoking marijuana all day had distorted our thinking and wishing that I had not stolen from Kmart, and now I was feeling like a poor victim in a bad situation, but I still believed that somehow Glenda would get us out of jail.

After what seemed to be several hours, I began to doubt my friend for the first time, so I began to speak up to her, saying, *"I want to go home, girl, so I'm gonna give them my momma's phone number."*

Glenda responded, saying, *"Stop it and be quiet!"* in a shallow but stern voice. She continued to say, *"They can hear you. We gon' get out of here! Just be patient. I got a plan!"* Glenda asked to use the phone and said that she had called a lady, and the lady she spoke to was coming to get us out. "So be quiet and wait!" she said. I tried to ask her questions about the mysterious lady, but she shushed me and looked at me with her eyes bucked, telling me to be quiet.

It started to seem like forever sitting in that small room, watching my friend Glenda shake the iron bars on the small window as though she were strong enough to break us out. It finally hit me that my friend didn't really have a plan at all, so I began to knock on the door, calling for the officer, shouting, "Hey, mister, hey, somebody!" Both my momma and Glenda's momma were there to get us really quick. I was sitting in the passenger side of the car listening to my momma fuss and threaten me with the beating I was going to be getting, and I was scared to say a word. All I could do was say a silent prayer, *"Lord, help me not to die tonight!"* Shortly after my experience in jail, we moved to another house only a few miles away from Glenda, so I could still hang out with her, and besides, we still went to the same school.

I met Antonio my last year at Brooks Junior High School. He lived just a couple of blocks over, and we quickly became friends. Antonio was thin and very tall, and he wore preppy clothes. They were always neatly pressed, and his shoes always matched whatever he wore, and when he talked, his eyes would blink at the same time, and he was the cutest boy I had ever seen other than my brothers, of course. Our bus rides to Cody High School were always fun even though the weather would sometimes be almost unbearable, but I looked forward to going to school with my friend. We would huddle up with the other kids like a football team as we waited for the bus in the depth of winter. In Detroit, the winters were brutal. It looked like Christmas during most of the wintertime, and sometimes after school, Antonio would come over to my house, and we would hang out in the basement and do karaoke, acting like I was Anita Baker and he was Marvin Gaye. It wasn't too long before Antonio and I were not only going to school together but skipping school and sometimes even coming back to my house after Momma went to work.

Antonio introduced me to a couple of adults that lived close to the school, and some days we would hang out in their apartment, getting high on marijuana and taking pills they called mescaline. Antonio had his secrets too, and they weren't much different than mine. We were both victims of molestation by grown-ups that we were supposed to trust! I couldn't understand the similarities because he was a boy, and I couldn't understand how a man could or why he would molest a boy. When I found out that my friend was having a sexual relationship with one of the adult males in the apartment and that he was gay as a result of his secrets, it made me even more angry at God, and my hate for men grew even more. What I still didn't realize at the time was that we were both using drugs and drinking because we didn't want to feel the pain anymore and that our secrets were destroying us both one smoke, one pill, and one drink at a time. I was also angry at the man in the apartment for messing with my friend, but I didn't know what to do or say. Antonio had trusted me with his secret, and I wouldn't dare betray him, and besides, I had too many secrets of my own to worry about his, so I decided I would just pretend he didn't tell me.

We were both young and dumb, and my friend was definitely being sexually abused by the adult male, but it seemed that Antonio liked it, and we were both being abused mentally and emotionally and enjoying that as well. I adored Antonio because he listened to me, and I could tell him anything. He reminded me of Glenda in some ways, but hanging out with him was more exciting than stealing at the local Kmart. He also reminded me of my brother Cedi when we were growing up because I could count on my brother to do anything I wanted him to. Even if it got us into trouble, he would do it.

As the years went by, I began to recreate myself based on my brokenness! I believe that when we don't receive new healthy information, our thoughts remain the same, and we *become* our thoughts. I hated myself enough to try and become someone else, and I despised men and resented my father because of my own inability to accept the things I could not change. My immaturity, anger, and my ignorance led me into some dangerous places. However, I wasn't afraid anymore. Instead, I was filled with false pride, and that word *love* was no longer in my vocabulary. Even the idea of love was distorted, and when someone said that word to me, it made me cringe. I didn't want to be loved because love had hurt me, so I didn't want anybody to love me ever again. Each day I woke up, I depended on my feelings, which had become my guidance, so whatever choices I made depended on how I felt that day. I didn't realize that my life was being led by the little-girl emotions, which had been violated and pushed aside for someone else's pleasure. I couldn't understand the sick mindset of a grown man, and I couldn't wrap my mind around how my momma would trust them with her kids. I swore to myself that I would never trust a man, not even my father. Besides, he had left before I could even meet him, so I considered him a deadbeat dad with the emphasis on dead anyway.

THE WINDY CITY

I was around fifteen years old when I met a new cousin, Loise. I can remember because I was going into the tenth grade. I was always excited to meet new family because in a desperate kind of way, I was always hoping for someone to rescue me from my pain and guilt. Loise was my momma's third cousin, and she lived in Chicago. She came to visit us one summer, and I could tell that she had a lot of money because of the way she talked. She was extra proper when she said, "Hello, darling, I'm your cousin, Loise," and I listened to every word she said as she talked down to Momma in a very arrogant kind of way. I was good at hearing what other people didn't hear, and I could hear her putting my momma down as she talked about her house while comparing our home to hers, saying things like, "My kitchen is much larger than this one!" or "I have three bathrooms, and I don't know how you live with only one bathroom with all these kids." But when she asked me if I wanted to come to Chicago and live with her followed by, "You can go to the high school in Chicago, and I will take you shopping," I never thought past the shopping, and it never even dawned on me that maybe my momma had talked to her about my behavior, and Loise had come to town to take me away and that she was planning to get me in line. I was just excited about someone wanting me, so I wanted to go live in Chicago. My only request was that Bria go with me. I could not live without her. She was my everything. She was the one who helped me when I was afraid, and even though she sometimes resented it, she still did it.

That year was a nightmare in itself. Loise was many things, but kind was not one of them. She had foster kids at her home when we came to live with her, a young girl whose name I can't recall and another preteen girl named Carla. I can remember a lady coming to the house one morning and taking the crying little girl away while she begged Loise not to let them take her. Carla was already a family member, which Loise had adopted from a cousin, and I think her momma was on drugs or in some way unfit to raise her, and her father, who had full custody, was closely related to Loise, so he had allowed for the adoption. On our first day at Loise's house, in walked a pretty young girl with big, beautiful dark eyes and thick, long hair. It was evident that she attended a Catholic school because she walked in wearing a plaid skirt, a pair of Mary Jane shoes, and a button-down shirt with a sweater. She had the prettiest eyes I had ever seen, big and innocent, and she was very polite. In a soothing tone, she said, "Hello," and I returned the greeting, "Hi."

I can also remember a short man that stayed in the home with Loise from time to time, who seemed very nice. After dinner, Loise asked Carla to show us to the basement, where Bria and I would be sleeping, and I thought, "This rich witch gon' put us in the basement?" but this basement was absolutely gorgeous, not like our basement in Detroit, where we danced and sang to Anita Baker and did our laundry at the same time. Her basement had carpet on the floor and a large bar like in a club, and it was heated, and besides, what choice did we have! Loise made sure we knew that this house had previously belonged to Muhammad Ali, but I didn't really care. I was just ready to get to the shopping. Somehow, I always thought the grass was greener on the other side.

Chicago was cold and windy! I didn't realize how cold it was until I had to take the bus to school. On our first day of school, Loise took my sister and I to school and showed us the bus stop to return home. She let us know right from the beginning that she was too busy to pick us up from school, so we would take the bus to and from school, saying, "I will meet you at home, and we will go shopping for clothes." Well, my idea of shopping and hers were completely different as we pulled up to Kresge, a store basically one step up from today's dollar stores. My jaw dropped, and the look on my face must have been very apparent. I didn't say much, but my facial expressions would tell it all every time when Loise looked at me with a God-awful look, saying, "Well, this is better than what you have!" She reminded me of that dark closet on Trowbridge Street that I was so afraid of, and I just knew that if I went into that closet, a monster would get me. Well, *the monster just got me*!

I was in Chicago with no clue of why I was really there in a new school in South Chicago called Bowen High, and this school was the biggest school I had ever seen. I was there in Chicago, me and the thing I always took with me, my fear, no matter where I went. At that point in my life, it didn't matter what I was afraid of or why I was afraid, whether it was the tennis-shoe man or my blindfold as I was left in the bathroom with a death threat, whether it was my stepdad, Rich, when he slammed his hand on the dinner table or going to the bathroom at night in fear of the dark. It didn't even matter anymore as fear had attached itself to me, and I was one big ball of living fear. But the difference now was that my fear was covered with false pride and anger, and I would dare any boy to look under my dress or any girl to try and fight me. I would just dare!

Although Loise proclaimed to be Catholic, I don't remember her going to church, but on one day a week, she would listen to a preacher, and I can remember hearing a preacher talk about fear and how it would contaminate faith, saying that fear is the total opposite of faith and that fear and faith cannot dwell in the same place, referring to it as oil and water! But as a teenager, I didn't know anything about faith. Besides, I don't know if I had even heard the word *faith*. In fact, there were a lot of words I had not heard, like "I'm sorry for hurting you" or "It's not your fault" or "I'm just a sick bastard, and it has nothing to do with you." My world had already been contaminated by the people that I was supposed to have faith in, and God had not been there to save me. So excuse me, Mr. Preacher Man, if I didn't have something I knew nothing about, and besides, everything about me was contaminated, so if you can't tell me what to do with that, then I don't want to hear your analogy.

Chicago didn't work out! Loise was a total witch, and I hated her guts. She drilled us like a sergeant in the military as she would force me to do homework at the kitchen table with Carla while comparing my work with a young child, saying things like, "I know you can do better than that, and it's shameful that Carla needs to help you with your homework." She even said to me that I was dumb, calling me "plain dumb." I once had an outer-body experience, visualizing putting her head in the pot of hot water that she was boiling to prepare that nasty dinner and stabbing her in the neck with the pencil that she forced me to write sentences with over and over again. I wanted so badly to tell her, "Witch, step off." Hell, half of the time I wasn't even present in school, at least not mentally. I wasn't used to this kind of abuse. This was definitely on another level. I was accustomed to getting my behind beat or slapped in the face for talking back to Momma and sent to bed, but this was mental torture. I wanted to go to school and learn, but I had a mental block, and it was a struggle getting new information into my brain. Nevertheless, I did my homework, went to school every day, and did my very best with what I had, but nothing was good enough for Loise. I watched her treat the many foster kids that came and went even worse. She treated them like garbage as she threw them away when she was done with them.

WAITING TO EXHALE

Momma came and got my sister and I and took us back to Detroit at the end of the school year in Chicago. I was so glad to be home I could have kissed the floor. Being home felt safe and familiar, and I couldn't wait for Momma to bake cookies so I could be in the kitchen to lick the bowl. My momma was so pretty, and I loved her so much, and I wanted to tell her about my pain, but I didn't know how to, and I hoped that she would someday ask me about my secrets, but she never did, and honestly, I'm not sure if she knew what to ask. I wanted her to just be with me and nobody else if only for a while. I wanted her to act like I was the only child she had, and I wanted her to hug me and tell me that everything would be okay because the trauma I had experienced was more alive than the first day it happened, and the fear had been magnified in all aspects of my life.

During that school year back home at Cody High School, I was supposed to be going into the eleventh grade because I had completed my tenth grade at Bowen High School in Chicago, but my transcripts were never found from Bowen High, and I didn't know what to do to get them. I was angry at Momma because I felt that she had let me down again, and I was resentful with the school system and embarrassed to have to complete the tenth grade all over again. I had worked hard under the pressure of Loise, and I didn't even skip school or smoke any marijuana, like my girlfriend did. I wanted Momma to be proud of me, and again I felt ignored and inadequate. I tried to stay in school for a while and even tried switching schools because I didn't want anyone to know I was a grade behind, but my insecurities and my fear kept me isolated let alone my secrets, which haunted me every day and every night.

That year I met George. He was my new guy friend and would ride the Chicago bus to school with me every morning along with Antonio. We all became really good friends, and the only difference was that George didn't have any secrets like Antonio and I had, but we had made a pact that we wouldn't tell him or anybody else our secrets. George was the tallest, darkest guy I had ever seen with the deepest voice I had ever heard, and he was so nice. He would show up just like Antonio, and we would all catch the bus together every morning, and of course, some days we would come back home after Momma went to work. George was a tough guy, and he was my protector, my big brother, and I knew that he cared about me a lot because when I was with George, I felt safe. When I think back, I often bonded with platonic male friends. Maybe that was God showing me that all men weren't bad.

I started back smoking marijuana, which made it nearly impossible to focus in school. Besides, I wasn't terribly interested in school anymore, and my grades dropped down to failing, and finally my pity party would get too big for me to handle, and I dropped out of school altogether.

I got my first job at the Jack in the Box restaurant, and I was happier than I had ever been because now I could buy what I wanted with my money, and I did. Every payday I went to the mall with my two buddies, Antonio and George. No one understood me like they did. They didn't judge me. Instead, they adored me and thought I was cool and cute, and I knew I was cute, but I didn't want any attention from the boys in any way except pure friendship. I thought about having a boyfriend from time to time, but I was too scared of the boys that wanted to date me and too insecure to tell anybody. Besides, I could be whoever I wanted to be with my guy friends, Antonio and George, because they accepted me just how I was, and that was all I needed.

Meme was a girl I met at Cody High School, and we clicked right away, and she became my girl, and we started hanging like wet clothes—and smoked a lot of marijuana. I liked Meme, but at times she could be very mean especially to her younger sister. I would often spend the night at her house and would witness her beating her little sister for talking back to her or anything that she didn't like. I think she resented the fact that every day after school, she would have to watch her until her momma came home. I can't help but think that maybe Meme was like Bria, resentful for having the responsibility for her little sister, so she beat on her because of her own frustration. She was also mean to some of her friends as well! I witnessed Meme literally throw a girl out of her car on the side of the road because she got smart with her, and on one occasion, she tried it with me, but my anger was just as big as hers, so I wasn't having it, so we argued all the way home. Meme would fight anybody anytime whenever she had to without hesitation. Although Meme and I smoked marijuana almost every day, I think I was a bit more into it than she was. Meme had dreams, and I didn't have any anymore. I just had my fear. She wanted to do hair and be an engineer, and me, I didn't want to be nothing anymore but free from fear. I didn't really like the way marijuana made me feel, but the fact that it made me feel different was good enough for me.

The next few years were party years. I was done with school, and I felt like a grown-up, making my own money and buying what I wanted, so I began to try the dating game. My first boyfriend was a boy in the neighborhood that I saw on the block from time to time named Vince. He was also a high school dropout who loved to drink and smoke marijuana, and he was very handsome, but when he drank, he would force himself on me, and although I didn't like it, I wouldn't resist. I didn't have any boundaries, and I didn't know how to establish any, so every time he would insist on having sex, I felt like that little girl all over again that was being violated. I felt powerless and helpless, but I wouldn't dare cry because tears never did anything for me except give me a headache and make my face red.

I was sixteen the first time I got pregnant by Vince, and I can remember Momma taking me to the doctor with me lying all the way there as she asked me over and over again, "Have you been having sex?"

"No, Momma, I haven't," I replied. I was afraid to tell her the truth. I was just embarrassed, and to me it wasn't sex; it never was. It was always rape, and I felt guilty all over again with another secret and another lie.

When the doctor came in with a sandwich in his hands, he looked like Columbo with a guilty verdict, "She's definitely pregnant!" I hid my face in shame as Momma looked at me in disgust without saying word. I could feel my throat drop to the bottom of my gut. I had done it again, something terribly bad, but Momma was emotionless as she and the doctor scheduled the appointment for my abortion without my permission.

I don't remember the conversation on the way home. I just remember silence in what seemed to be the longest car ride in history. Momma had already told us girls early on that if we had a baby, we had to get our own house because she was not raising any more kids. I remember waking up in the hospital after the abortion, thinking, "Did they just kill my baby?" No one had asked me what I wanted to do about this baby. No one came and hugged me and said, "I'm sorry about your loss." No one talked to me about counseling or any other option to express how I felt, and Momma's only words were, "We don't need to talk about this ever again." I had just had another experience with trauma!

Trauma is defined as a deeply distressing or disturbing experience. It was something that I had been experiencing over and over again, and it happens in the lives of many without much concern, especially in the lives of young girls and young boys. In the years to come, abortions would be something that I would experience again and again, so many that I lost count. Those would definitely have been classified as trauma events, and I would probably need therapy for them all; however, I stuffed those feelings in my bag after every abortion and kept it moving.

THE BAG LADY

Al was a boy I had seen around the way at Cody High School, but I don't think he ever noticed me because he seemed to be very popular, and I was nobody. I never talked to any boy in high school except for Antonio and George, and besides, I wasn't there long. I believe I was around seventeen when we started dating, and I had already dropped out of school. Al was a few years older than I was, and he was tall and handsome, and he always made me laugh. I liked everything about him, and I knew he liked me too because he treated me nice and never made me feel bad or hurt me physically. I thought I finally found someone that really cared for me, and maybe one day we could get married. I never dated a boy in high school and never wanted to, and my relationship with Vince had been over since the abortion, and I had decided that I would never date a drunken fool again.

When Al and I started dating, I felt like I was the luckiest girl in the world. We went out to parties together, and he was not ashamed of me, and my self-esteem rose to an all-time high! I was happy for the first time in my life, and I trusted him so much that I became dependent on him to keep me happy. I didn't know anything about codependency at the time, but I was definitely experiencing an unhealthy clinginess, and Al was all I needed to feel good and be happy. Al and I smoked marijuana together, and he also introduced me to a new drug called cocaine, and we did a line from time to time, but I didn't need marijuana or cocaine to make me feel good or different. All I needed was Al, so I only did cocaine when we were together. I enjoyed having sex with him because it was different. He never forced me or made me feel bad afterward. Instead we would spend many hours afterward talking.

When Al got married, my heart was broken, and although I knew he had started seeing someone else, it didn't ease the pain. I had even seen him in parties with another girl, but we never talked about it, and when we were together, I never asked him about it because he told me that he loved me, and that was all I needed. Honestly, that should have been a red flag because when someone said they loved me, it was their own definition, not mine. I didn't trust love. It had hurt me in the past, but this seemed different coming from Al. It didn't feel wrong or distorted. Instead, it felt genuine, and I loved him back. But I soon came to find that love didn't have much to do with commitment or honesty! My heart was broken into many pieces when I found out that he had married another girl, and I could feel the hurt so deep down inside, but I dared not cry. Instead as usual, I stuffed that broken heart right in my bag along with the guilt, shame, embarrassment, resentment, fear, and anger, and I moved right along.

I returned like a dog with her tail tucked between her legs back to what I knew best: fear, anger, and resentment. I began to smoke marijuana more and experiment with other drugs, and sex with guys was like a walk in the park because I didn't have any more feelings about boys whatsoever. It all felt the same, and most of the time it felt like rape. In fact, there were a few times when it could definitely have been classified as rape because I would say no in a subtle, scared, shaky voice, and the guy would push himself on me anyway, but I was too scared to resist, and the drugs and drinking on top of that would render me defenseless, and although inside I would be screaming, "No!" my body would be saying something different, like, "I'm defenseless and all yours. Do what you want with me!" I allowed men to use me like a toilet, and when it was over, I tried to flush those feelings, but just like those panties I had tried to flush, those feelings were always floating around on the surface, and I wore them like a badge. I didn't understand how sexual abuse had affected me, and I was ashamed of myself after every sexual encounter, and every abortion would leave me in a depressed state with another empty space in my soul.

I once heard that God knows everything about us, and I often wondered if God really knew me or the things that had transpired in my life or if He did not care enough to help me, and if He did care, why didn't He protect me when I was an innocent child and could not protect myself? I didn't understand God, and I didn't think He understood me either, and I surely didn't feel protected by Him! I was taught that if you were good, you would go to heaven and be with God, but if you were bad, you would go to hell, where you would burn forever, so I was afraid of God just as much as I was of any other man, and besides, there wasn't much good in me, so I had no plans of going to heaven, and if God was a man, I didn't stand a chance anyway, so what was the point?

DRESSED-UP GARBAGE CAN

At the age nineteen, I became a backup singer for a local artist TJ Brooks. He was quite popular in the local clubs in Detroit, and he did lots of nightclub gigs. I loved to sing and dance, and to perform on stage was the thing that I knew I did well. As a child I had dreams of acting and singing opera, but many of my dreams were pretty foggy by this time. I had built up so many resentments because I felt like many things had been taken away from me. My body was taken at a very young age. The school system had denied me the right to be promoted to the eleventh grade. Another woman had stolen Al from me, and of course, my father had left me fatherless, and I was definitely playing the blame game! But singing and dancing was something I could do, and no one could take that away from me.

Meme and I were both in the singing group, and at one time we had two other girls that made the group even hotter. We practiced quite often and would perform in the local clubs with TJ Brooks. I really thought we were going to be big stars, but a little bit of drama always interfered because someone was angry with someone most of time about something, and of course, there were going to be drama when drugs were involved. I remember my friend Keith saying, "Find the drugs, find the drama." TJ wasn't just a singer. He was also a drug dealer, and he was supplying us with cocaine during the rehearsals and the shows, saying, "This here will get you going," and since we were all sexy black women, we became associated with his drug ring really quick. Of course, they were all men with lots of drugs and money, so when TJ didn't have what we needed, we knew where to go. I knew I was gorgeous, and I could dress myself up like a movie star, not to mention my gift of gab, and I could talk any man out of almost anything, and if they didn't fall for my gift of gab, hell, I was taking it anyway because I had many tricks up my sleeve. Besides, my best friend Antonio had taught me how to put a man to sleep with a little Visine in his liquor, which I never had to use that trick because most men liked to drink when they got high on cocaine, so that would usually knock them out anyway.

I knew I was getting high way too often. Even Meme would criticize me from time to time, saying, "*Girl, you getting high too much. You might want to chill out!*" I despised her for saying that to me, but I knew she was right, and I tried to be like her and go to school, but I had not gotten my high school diploma, so I felt inadequate under her.

I started hanging out with Robin. She was a girl I had met through Meme, and her boyfriend was a drug dealer, so most of the time she had plenty of drugs and parties at her house, and I was present for most of them. Since Meme couldn't keep up with me, Robin became my girl, but she had two boys and was struggling to support them, so she turned tricks on the weekends for money, and I was attracted to her strength and courage to do what she needed to do for her kids. I tried turning tricks couple of times to get money, but I was too afraid that a john would kill me, and I felt disgusted and sick to my stomach every time I would come out of a hotel room with a man I didn't know! Robin had grown up in the projects on the east side of Detroit, and her momma was a heroin addict, and on several occasions, she cried about it, saying that she wanted her kids to have a better life than she and her siblings had, so she decided to enlist in the Army, asking me if I would go with her on the buddy plan.

I wasn't accepted into the Army since I didn't have my high school diploma, and as I watched Robin make plans to leave her boys with her aunt and prepare to go to the military, I began feeling alone and lost again, and although I didn't really want to go to the Army, it was Robin's idea, and it sounded like a good one at the time, and I was always searching for that next best thing or the next person to change my life because my dreams had pretty much been shattered, and the fact that the military denied me created another feeling of worthlessness to add to my bag.

Eventually I got my GED, and I felt like my life was headed into a different direction, and I was feeling really proud of myself. I got my second job working at the liquor store on Seven Mile in Detroit, and that's where I met El! He would come into the store almost every day and buy a very expensive bottle of champagne. Sometimes he wasn't alone, but still he would smile at me and tell me how pretty I was, and as he would drive out of the parking lot in his red Corvette, I would glance out thinking, "Damn!" El was dark-skinned, muscular, well-groomed, and fine! And when he asked me for my phone number, I was overjoyed. El worked at General Motors and had his own apartment in Southfield, and I thought I had found my husband, the man that would really help me get my life together. But it wasn't long before I found out that El wasn't just working at General Motors. He was also dealing cocaine, but the fact that he dressed in expensive clothes and bought expensive champagne was more apparent than his side job, and I was impressed.

I moved in with El only after a couple of months dating, and he would cook some amazing meals, which I loved because I didn't like to cook. He would tell me stories about his upbringing in Long Island, New York, telling me that his father was a doctor and his momma was an attorney, and when he would talk about them, he always had a huge smile on his face so much that I could tell he missed his family. El had five brothers, and all of them had successful careers, and he would laugh when he talked about the fights he and his brothers had growing up. Eventually I did get the opportunity to meet one of his brothers, and his best friend from New York came to visit us a couple of times, but I was never graced with the opportunity to meet his parents, but from the stories that El would share with me, I felt like I knew his whole family anyway.

El was not just a drug dealer but a drug addict as well, and I'm sure he didn't know just as I didn't that the road we were traveling was leading us both to hell. I always thought that men were stronger and bigger than women and that they didn't feel pain. El had a lot of important friends even some who hung out with a big-time professional boxer from Detroit. His friends all got high on cocaine and drank expensive champagne, so I began to use with them as well.

When I was high on coke, I felt special and on top of the world, and when I was with El, I felt important, and I was impressed with all the things he had going on in his life, and he was a perfect gentleman at least in the beginning of our relationship.

I'd had a few experiences with cocaine with my ex-boyfriend Al, and I was using powder cocaine quite a bit with TW's crew, but something different was about to happen! El introduced me to a new way to get high called freebasing, which was cooking cocaine and smoking it out of a pipe. It was the most amazing high I had ever experienced. I felt like I had died and gone to drug heaven. At first, I was afraid because this new high was just too good to be true! It took me so far away from reality and created an escape from all my troubles, and I think I was hooked immediately, so much that I couldn't see that a big truck was coming, and I was standing in the middle of the road.

Our relationship went south really quick after my introduction to the devil himself, freebase cocaine. El and I began using so often that we both knew we were getting high too much, so we tried to control it by only using on the weekend and once in a while during the week, but our attempts to control this monster were in no way successful. El became his own biggest customer, and before long, the money from his drug sales outside of his regular paycheck was a thing of the past. Once the drug use got bad, the other El came out. Dr. Jekyll died, and Mr. Hyde came out with a vengeance! He was stressed when we couldn't get high, and when we did, we would fight—at least he fought me! He would knock me to the floor so quick without notice that I wouldn't see it coming. Usually, it was over drugs or at least the behavior we had adopted from our drug use. I just wanted a man that would care for me, but at the time I was blindsided and tricked by the enemy. The devil knows how to use our weaknesses to destroy us especially when we don't know who we are or who we belong to. I was like a backpacker going wherever the next ride would take me, defenseless and confused, like when El would hit me and afterward say he was sorry followed by the old familiar, "I love you!"

I didn't want to use drugs or to fight about drugs anymore, but by this time I was in full-fledged addiction, and I had started crossing all boundaries and morals that I had been taught as a young girl. I didn't understand what was going on in my life, and I didn't know how to stop it or even deal with it, so I just continued using with El and allowing him to treat me like crap. I was young and dumb and living in a world that I didn't even understand. No one had told me how to handle this type of relationship. In fact, no one had told me how to handle *any* relationship. I don't remember Momma saying much about boys at all except to stay away from them, and here I was with a grown man seven years older than I was with many possessions, and I had become one of them. El would apologize after every slap or every disrespectful act, and I would accept his apology.

One night, El's friend came over with two females. The friend took his girl into the guestroom, and El said to me, "I'll be back. I need to talk to her," taking the other girl into our bedroom as I was sitting in the living room watching TV. When they finally came out of the bedroom, it was the next morning. I just sat in the living room all night long crying inside because I would never let any man see me cry. I had secretly cried one time since I was twelve years old, and that was when Al got married, but there were no tears to come out. They were all inside drowning me one cry and one scream at a time. I was paralyzed, and I didn't know what to think or do as my thoughts go from hurt feelings to psychotic. I thought of walking into the bedroom, asking, "What's going on?" as if I didn't know to setting the entire apartment on fire. Instead, I walked away that morning, got into to my car, and stuffed my bag with yet another feeling called dumbass.

I was still hanging out with the band and performing in nightclubs, and I was just about over El's crap, but I couldn't leave I didn't know if it was my own abandonment issues or my codependency, so I decided if I was going stay with him and continue to get high that I would get my own drugs! I started hanging out all night whenever and with whomever I wanted, and I began giving El the same disrespect he had been giving me, and when he would get mad and start yelling, I would punch him in his face before he could get his last word out. At least I would get one good hit in, and I didn't care if he kicked my butt or not. This dude didn't know how much anger I had inside and how much trauma I had experienced as a result of abuse from men, but he was about to find out. No more slaps in my face without consequences, and if there was going to be a fight, we both were going to be in it. Sometimes El would be so shocked by my punch that he would just back off, saying, "Girl, you got a damn problem." I was so over this loser, and as result, he put me out of his apartment completely by taking my clothes and dropping them off at my momma's house.

GEOGRAPHICAL CHANGE

In 1985, I moved to Chattanooga, Tennessee, which was where I was born, looking for a place of refuge with hopes of changing my own life with the same thinking that I had messed it up with. In a new town with new people to take advantage of, I was searching for some new ideas. Maybe I would go back to school and could get my life together here in a smaller town, where no one knew me, but I was still living in my pain, and although I had low self-esteem, I knew I was still young and pretty with lots of guys looking my way. Of course, I would soon find a drug dealer to feed the monster that had only been temporarily arrested, but I did well for a while with my plan to work all week and party on the weekends. I began hanging out at a local club called Scopus, and that's where I met my girlfriend Tee. She worked there as a waitress, and she was cool as hell. At first, I didn't know how to talk to her because when she spoke to me, she often referred to me using the *b* word. Now that was definitely not how we talked to a friend in Detroit! If you called someone the *b* word or said "Yo momma," you would most likely end up in a fight, but Tee had grew up in Boston, and that's how they talked, so I quickly got used to her language because I knew she didn't mean it in a bad way.

I started working with a local band in Chattanooga because I still wanted to sing and perform. That was the thing other than drugs that would take my mind away from everything else. I was somebody when I was on the stage, and when I was high and on stage, I had all the courage I needed to transform myself. To be honest, I was a coward, a scared little girl all the time, so alcohol and drugs providing me with an escape if only for a while was good enough for me.

I never felt a part of anything, but being on stage set me free, and everyone in the audience loved me and accepted me in the moment. They didn't know my secrets, and they didn't care. The problem was that I couldn't stay on stage long enough to erase my past, and my drinking and drug use was starting to get out of hand again. When I'd wake up the next morning with a hangover, sometimes I couldn't even remember the show, like the time I forgot the words to the song because I was too drunk, and when I did remember how I had embarrassed myself, I would just put another drug on it and hold on to my pride, pulling out one of my masks, cover up my face, and keep it moving, acting like I wasn't bothered by it at all. I had many masks, and I had become very good at changing scenes. Hell, I was always acting because I didn't trust anyone or anything, and I definitely didn't trust love, and I didn't want anybody to say that word to me ever again in life. I decided I would just love myself and keep all that other toxic love away from me, so I decided to love myself to death, literally.

One night, while performing in a local talent show, I looked up, and there he was—Dee! He was definitely a sight for sore eyes—tall, light-skinned, and gorgeous! I don't think I ever saw any man that looked like my dad until I saw him. He reminded me of the military picture, the only one I had ever seen of Julian, my daddy. *"Who is that?"* I asked my friend Tee.

"Girl, that's Dee. You don't wanna mess with him!"

I didn't even ask why. I just knew at that moment that I had to have him. I was already dating Jay, but whatever, that didn't matter. One was too many, and a thousand was never enough. Besides, I was no one's girlfriend. I liked them all, and as long as they were giving me what I wanted and not punching me around, it was all good, and what they thought didn't matter. I felt as though all men were dirty, low-down scumbags, and if they wanted to be in my company, then it came with a price tag, and I wasn't cheap! Hell, men had already taken what they wanted from me and sent me on my way, like I was an old shoe, not a real person with feelings—just a little fat girl that sucked her finger and craved the attention of her momma that she never got. The tables had turned. I was tall and slim with long hair and an attitude, and if I wanted it, I was getting it one way or another, and if you wanted me, then put your money on the table or get the hell out!

Dee and I basically had a "sex-ship." I don't remember us ever having a girlfriend-and-boyfriend talk. Besides, we didn't talk much at all about anything. Instead, we would usually meet at the club and leave together, and he would come to my house for sex, or I would go to his parents' house, where he lived at the time. I never had the opportunity to meet them until I found out I was pregnant—for real this time. See, I had claimed to be pregnant on several occasions just to get abortion money because Dee was a hard one to crack when it came to money. I liked his company, but he was stingy as hell, so I would often lie to get money from him. Oh, I was getting that money one way or another! That was the only way I could feel better about sleeping with him or any man for that matter.

I wasn't sure if he cared about me or not. I just knew we had a lot of fun together, and because I could do what I wanted with him and see him whenever I wanted to, I felt a bit in control. I always felt used and abused by men, especially after sex, and I would usually pretend to be someone else, like a movie star on TV, to keep it from feeling like rape or me feeling like a victim. But it was my own low self-esteem, low self-worth, and shame that would still cause the same feelings afterward. Somehow making them pay was a way to justify them touching me and a way for me to feel some kind of dignity. I wasn't worth much to me, but I'll be damned if I was going to be treated that way by any man anymore! I knew that men valued money more than life or any woman, so I was for sale at the right price, and that was the way I controlled them.

No more El to punch me whenever he felt like it, no more drunk Vince forcing himself on me, and no more Al leaving me at the altar for a real wedding with another woman that didn't even deserve him! My anger was nasty, and I was over being treated like I didn't matter or like I was someone else's temporary punching bag. There were so many secrets that I was carrying around that I was overloaded. I was the bag lady, and my bags were getting too heavy for me! The problem was that instead of putting the bags down, I kept stuffing them with more guilt, more secrets, and more shame.

At age twenty-seven, I found out that I was pregnant. I had so many mixed emotions, such as excitement, joy, and of course, fear. I had already had several abortions, and I was reluctant to get one with this child. At the same time I didn't want my kid to come into a world that was filled with pain, so I pondered until it was too late to get an abortion, and then it hit me that I was a drug addict, so how would I be a mom and use drugs at the same time? As my child started to grow inside of me, I began to feel a love that I had never felt before, so I did it. I gave up the drugs long enough to give birth to a healthy, beautiful baby girl, and when I saw her, I knew that I loved her more than life. I planned to be the best mom I could be, but after being in the hospital for a few days, my addiction began to hunt me, and fear came in like thunder and a rushing wind, and I had drugs delivered to my hospital room. I tried my best to take care of my baby girl, but I was so overwhelmed I couldn't stop thinking about my past, and I couldn't sleep, and although it was just me and her in my home, my anxiety would not let me rest. Instead, I needed to watch her at night to make sure no one would come in and bother her, and only after a year or so, my family began to express their concerns about my parenting and would eventually intervene.

I was in so much denial that I had convinced myself that I could handle it, and when my momma would share her concerns about the safety of my daughter, I would often respond in anger, saying, "I love my baby, and I would never allow anything bad to happen to her!" God knows I loved my baby with everything in me. Unfortunately, there wasn't much in me operating from a place of love! The real truth was that I was an addict from the pit of my soul, addicted to fear, anger, and drugs, and I desperately needed a solution. I was trying my best to be a good momma with a broken spirit, so I continued to use drugs and money to make me feel better and to cover my shame. I was like a train headed the wrong way on the tracks, not realizing that I would eventually crash. Nevertheless, nothing was more important than getting my feel better, and that was my painful reality.

Dee still lived with his parents, and I wanted to be the one to tell his momma that she had a grandchild. I had hoped that she would invite me over so she could see the baby, and I hoped she was the mom that would say, "I'm sorry my son is treating you this way." I hoped she would cry with me, but instead, I felt like a total fool and a one-night stand when I got off the phone with her as she said to me in a stern but sophisticated voice, "Take care of your own problem. I took care of mine!"

I didn't mean any harm, but I regretted that I had called her. I felt like that sixteen-year-old girl all over again when my momma took me to the doctor for that first abortion. I felt like she was ashamed of me when she made me vow not to discuss the abortion anymore. I looked at my beautiful baby girl, and strength and courage rose up inside of me like never before, and I promised her that no one would ever hurt her, or I would definitely kill them, and I meant every word of it! I just didn't know at the time that it would be me that would be the one hurting her by not being available for her year after year. I didn't know that my drug use would get so bad that I wouldn't be able to read bedtime stories to her and that it would soon be my momma stepping in to be her mom.

I didn't know that I would become so angry that someone else was more equipped to support my child physically and emotionally than I was and how angry I would be with my momma and would question her motives for taking my child from me to protect her from me, her real momma, when she didn't even protect me, her own child. How dare she tell me what to do with my child when her daughter was a grown woman with little-girl emotions, and she didn't have a clue of the pain that was haunting me, and I couldn't tell her because I was trying to protect her and that the only relief I could find was in a bottle or a crack pipe. I just didn't know!

VICTIM TO VICTIMIZER

In 1990, I had a new baby and a new dude. I knew it was definitely over with Jay because he hated me and was trying to sue me for the $1,000 baby bed that he had gotten for my baby, which he wasn't getting. Dee and I were getting ready to go to court over child support, and he knew he wasn't going to touch me ever again especially after he questioned me about paternity, but honestly, I didn't expect anything short of disappointment from any man. I knew that men were just men. All of them were the same kind of cowards by my definition. I still hated them all, and I used them for what I needed, and I felt used by them because they always got what they wanted. So I stuffed all those feelings and emotions I received from Dee and his momma along with the regret of hurting James by having a baby by another man right into my bag with all the other feelings and moved right along.

    I met Rose in Huntsville, Alabama, at a nightclub where I went with one of my girlfriends, Josey. I had met her while hanging out with a club promoter by the name of Jay-D. Well, of course, he was also a drug dealer! We were visiting his parents in Alabama. Josey lived in Alabama as well, and she and I would oftentimes go to Huntsville to party. One night while sitting in the club with her having drinks and shooting the breeze as Josey called it, a guy across the room began sending drinks over to our table, and after a few rounds in walked an older guy with glasses not very tall with a goofy kinda look on his face with an introduction he must have been practicing all night as we drank on his tab: "Hello, ladies, I'm Rose," he said. "You all having a good time?"

We both responded with silly laughter with a nod, saying yes, and thanked him for the drinks, waiting for him to ask if he could join us as he began taking a seat at the same time asking if he could join us. We both giggled a bit and said sure. Besides, he was paying for the drinks.

At the end of the night, he leaned over to me and gave me his card, saying, "Call me." I responded I might. He responded back, "You will!" Wow, this dude was an arrogant prick! Josey and I laughed all the way home about it.

A week or so later, Josey and I were talking, and she asked me if I had called Rose, and I said, "Girl no, I'm not calling that old man!"

Josey responded, saying, "Well, the word is that he got fat pockets, and I heard that he's big time in Huntsville." She went on to say, "I don't know what he does, but I heard 'round the club that he got it going on!"

I replied, "Hmm."

One day while cleaning my house, I came across the card that I had gotten from Rose, the guy in the club in Alabama, and I laughed at the thought of his statement that I would call him. I was a new momma and handling my business quite well, and although I was still getting high, I was holding it together, which I could usually do for a while. I had lost all my baby fat in the hospital after four days, so I have to admit that I was still a hot number, so I thought what could it hurt, so I called him.

"I've been thinking about you," Rose said as he answered the phone in a smooth voice. "How are you?" he asked.

"I'm good, just taking care of my baby."

"Oh, you have a baby, and how's that relationship?" I paused, not expecting that question as he quickly responded to my hesitation, saying, "If you have a baby, then there must be a father!"

I replied, answering his question with a question, "What about you? Do you have any kids?"

He quickly replied, "Yes, and a wife!"

I wasn't serious about anyone, so the fact that he was married didn't matter. However, I was a bit surprised at his level of transparency, but the fact that he was so forthcoming was impressive. See, no man had my full undivided attention, and I was only calling him out of curiosity, so the fact that he was married really didn't matter.

I had been struggling with the cost of repairs of my car and was talking to Rose about maybe purchasing a new car, and a week later, he showed up with a brand-new Nissan Sentra—candy-apple red! I was highly impressed because no man had ever treated me so kind. Rose played a lot of golf, and on many occasions, he would invite me to travel with him to his golf trips. I would pack up my daughter and travel with him, staying in the finest hotels, eating the best food, and shopping at some of the biggest malls, and I loved it. The problem was that I didn't love him, and he was falling for me headfirst!

We were spending so much time together that I couldn't help wonder about his wife and what she must have been thinking about his time away, so I asked, "How is it that you have this much freedom?" He told me that he and his wife were having problems, and I thought, "I guess so. You're dating another woman, but what did I care?"

I was getting what I wanted, so I just listened as he explained that neither of them had been happy for many years, and quickly he asked a question, one that I was not prepared for, "If I get a divorce, will you marry me?"

I knew not to agree to this kind of crap, but I had never taken any man for his word anyway, so I said with very little sincerity, "Sure."

I was busy working and taking care of my baby girl and hanging out in my new car as often as I could. I worked the midnight shift at the baking company, and it was an okay job except I had been trying to get off the night shift since I started. I would show up at the club on my weekends off to meet my girlfriend Tee and sometimes her sister Trey, which I adored as well, and we would have a ball. She was just as beautiful as Tee. But Tee had two kids by this time, so it wasn't easy to get to the club, so sometimes we would meet up at her house or mine. I can say that those were the good using days. I was young and beautiful, and I had beautiful girlfriends and lots of dudes looking my way, but at the end of the day I still had that bag full of feelings that would haunt me daily.

I had been in Chattanooga about four years now, still working at the baking company, and I was getting so tired of the midnight shift, and the fact that I was using more didn't make it any easy to keep my eyes open all night long, so I had started using on the job at nights to stay awake, which eventually would lead to missing way too many work nights. Eventually, I was given the final ultimatum by management, which was to either resign or be fired. My baby girl was almost a year old when I found myself unemployed.

Rose and I were in an okay place, at least I thought so, but my attitude about him was, "You can hang around and give me what I want, or you can disappear," so as long as he let me have my way, we were good. I had turned him down on the proposal after he showed up with his divorce papers. I was not getting ready to marry a man twenty years older than I was. In fact, I had given up any idea of marriage since Al had married another woman and left me at my own altar. Rose was a sincere guy, and I really did like him, but I didn't respect him or any other man, so I used him, and I did not care how he felt about it. I didn't know how to make anything work with a man because I was stuck in my pain and resentments. I was sick from the abuse, and I didn't know that God was the only one that could heal me and open my eyes to a new way of life. All I knew was that all men owed me something, and I was collecting.

BACK IN MY CITY

I was unemployed and packing to move back to Detroit because there was no reason for me to stay in Chattanooga. I no longer had a job and had started using way too often, and I was getting a little scared about it, and I was still dealing with the court in regards to child support. I wasn't happy in Chattanooga anymore. I was beginning to experience feelings of depression, so I decided to go home back to Detroit, my old familiar where my family was and where I knew I could make it, so Rose rented a truck and drove me back to Detroit. I was a momma for the first time, and I loved my daughter so much. She was my little baby doll in the flesh. I dressed her up every day, and she was such a happy and healthy baby, but now I was back in Detroit, where it all started, with no clue about this thing that was lurking around in my mind and in my flesh. I did what a momma would do—got a place to live for me and my baby and decorated it with my own things that Rose and I had brought from Chattanooga. When Rose drove out of my driveway in the huge moving truck, I felt like my father was leaving me again, and I knew it was over. I could see the look on his face as he said goodbye to me, and I could feel his disappointment. I knew it was the end of our relationship as we had known it to be, not that it was super healthy or based on any solid foundation. Instead, it was as toxic as I was. The truth was that Rose had signed up to be a daddy, my daddy, and he didn't even know it.

I started to hang out again with my guy friend Antonio, and we started doing what we always did, getting high, but this time it was different because crack cocaine had hit the streets in Detroit, and I had not a clue of what this new drug would cost me. Antonio told me that it was a lot cheaper than buying cocaine and that it was much easier to get, so I tried it, and oh my God, it took my mind to the moon and back so fast that I couldn't help but want more. I felt like I was chasing a car that had all my belongings in it and was not going to stop until I caught up to that car. I had met the devil freebasing with El and decided that I would not touch a pipe again in life, and I hadn't for about five years. Now this was the devil's daddy, and unbeknownst to me, this drug would cost me more than money—it would steal my life from me! I didn't know that my entire life was at stake and that I would sell my soul to get just one more hit, and that one more would never ever be enough.

Meme and I also started hanging out again as well, and she was also doing crack, and many nights, things got really serious. Finding ways and means to get more was not always an easy task or a safe one for that matter. I was the one most of the time who would act out of desperation, sometimes stealing the drugs from the dope man and putting our lives in danger. My addiction spun out of control really quick, and Meme and I both were doing things to get high that went against the morals that had been instilled in us. When I was under the influence, I didn't see danger, just an opportunity to get what I needed to feel what I needed to feel. I was on crack now, and once I got that first hit, there was nothing or no one that could stop me from doing whatever I needed to do to get that next hit. Lord knows I was in many situations that could have killed me or someone else, and although I was scared out of my mind, I couldn't leave until I got what I needed. I would definitely have some moments of clarity and think about my baby and my life, but it seemed as though the guilt of it would drive me deeper into desperation, so more drugs would be the solution.

REHAB LIFE

A couple of years after my daughter was born, I was introduced to a twelve-step program by my stepsister, Ronny. She had been clean for many years, so I was open to trying it. This program gave me some information that I had never even thought about. The blue book that's read in the twelve-step program described addiction as a disease and that this disease was spiritual in nature, and the meetings provided a place for me talk about my feelings openly and to listen to others as they shared their own personal traumas. People in the rooms identified themselves as addicts and would say things like "*Feelings are just feelings*" and that feelings couldn't kill us. Instead, it's what we did with the feelings that would have the most impact. I also found that many addicts had experienced the same kind of trauma that I had and could identity with my pain. People in the meetings would often share how they had found hope and freedom as a result of attending meetings, and I could hear the chairperson saying that the only requirement for membership was the desire to stop using and that any addict could stop using, lose the desire to use, and find a new way to live.

Old-timers were the addicts that had a lot of clean time and would often approach me after the meeting to tell me that if I worked the program and trusted in a higher power to restore me to sanity, I could gain freedom from active addiction as well. However, in my mind I wasn't an addict, and I was not going to tack another title on to my already flawed personality. I was a victim, not an addict, and I only came to the meetings because my family didn't understand me and thought that I had a problem with drugs. Well, maybe I did get high too often, but I didn't believe that being in a meeting with a roomful of people calling themselves addicts would make a difference, so after a few months or so, I stopped attending the meetings because I was more comfortable living in my feelings and allowing them to dictate my every action, and I definitely wasn't ready to tell my secrets to a room full of people that I didn't know. Besides I didn't want to be an addict! Why should I be considered a sick addict? I didn't rape or molest kids or anyone else. No, I want the *mofos* dead, and I want to live to see them suffer—end of story!

The first rehab was a religious one, so we had to attend church on Sundays and do Bible study during the week, and it was suggested that we confess our sins pray every day. I knew how to pray because my grandma had taught us to say our prayers at night, and my auntie would pray with us, but to be confessing my sins was a bit overwhelming. Besides, didn't God already know what I had done and what had been done to me? I felt like I was reliving my trauma all over again, leaving me not only sick to my stomach but also angry.

Let me just say that I was good at conforming to someone else's belief system probably because I didn't have one of my own. I wasn't sure that God would do anything for me, and actually I didn't even like God, and I didn't think He liked me either. I just hoped that He cared enough to help me get clean and figure out a better way to live instead of the desperate way that I was living, so I followed the rules and began to pray.

I graduated the program, and now I had a church and a God that had cured me, but the problem was I didn't really believe. It was someone else's belief in this God that I knew nothing about, but I wanted to trust God especially when I would hear the stories about how God had delivered other people, but I couldn't stop wondering why He would allow men to abuse little kids and do whatever they wanted to and get away with it. I was confused at how this God could be both good and bad. Maybe that's why I was good sometimes and other times so bad. Maybe I was just like Him. I still had those feelings of fear, and I was afraid that the pain deep down in my gut was waiting for me to come home to torment me all over again, and I still had my secrets, and no one asked me what they were. They just told me that God could handle any issue that I had and that I was healed by His stripes. I believed it as long as I was in rehab, but when I returned home, it was like trying to hold on to a slippery pole! That voice in my head quickly returned and would tell me I needed something to make me feel better, to quiet those thoughts in my head, and to take away the fear that I would feel every night that caused me to tremble in my bed.

    I would walk the floor at night to check on my daughter to make sure she was safe because the trauma of my abuse had caused me to be paranoid. I couldn't let no one hurt her like I had been hurt, and I would kill for her safety or die trying. I would try my best to pray to that God from rehab, but the voices in my head and the visions that would follow would make me afraid to go to sleep at night. I just knew someone was going to come into my house and rape me and try to hurt my child, so I had to be on guard at all times.

    At one point using was not even a choice. It just became a part of my life, and I needed something to keep me sane, but the thing that helped me escape was the same thing that was ruining my life one drug at a time, one pill at a time, and one drink at a time, and my life got darker and darker. I went in and out of drug rehab centers. I even checked myself in to a few mental hospitals, trying to find a cure for my seemingly fatal problem, but failure was the result of my many attempts—over and over again!

    My family was trying to help me, but they didn't know what to do. So to take my child away from me out of their fear that something would happen to her as a result of my drug use was their way of forcing me to clean up my act. But it didn't work! By 1996, I had pretty much lost all I had except my man! Well, truth was, I had pretty much lost him too because he didn't have any respect for me, but I think he didn't want to completely abandon me, so he would come by to give me a few dollars here and there, but I knew he didn't understand and was tired of my mess. There was just a bit of hope that I held on to, and there was that fight in me that I believe I got from my grandma. I knew deep down inside that using drugs was not my destiny and that there was something better for me, and I knew that my life was not supposed to be this way, and every time I did something degrading to get drugs, I could feel a piece of my soul being ripped right out of my body. I didn't know God, and I didn't think He cared for me, but I knew there was something there protecting me because when I would tremble at night crying inside, I could feel a comforting presence rocking me to sleep, and when I was on somebody's couch or in a bed that reeked with bad odors or walking the street with nowhere to go, I felt protected.

Mister was my hero, and he never gave up on me, and even if he did at some point, he still would come and find me and take me home or somewhere to make sure I was safe. One morning after I had been in God knows whose house for several days and homeless for weeks, he showed up and demanded I leave with him, taking me to Herman Kiefer Hospital in another attempt to get me clean. Lord knows I was tired! I wanted so bad to stop using and to sleep in a clean place, and I was so tired of not being able to take a hot shower in a clean bathtub. I was so hungry and weak that I could hardly stand up. I wanted to see my baby and hold her in my arms and kiss her and tell her how much I loved her and how sorry I was for not being a good momma. I wanted something different, and I was so tired of being angry. I was sick and tired of being sick and tired!

A NEW LIFE

I was sent to New Life Treatment Center for drug rehab on the east side of Detroit, which was ran by two women who had both been in recovery themselves for many, many years. I was given a counselor named Emma, and she was also in recovery. I can remember sitting in front of her doing my intake and answering questions when she asked me why I was there and what I wanted to accomplish. I wasn't sure what she meant because clearly this was rehab for drug addiction, so I said that I wanted to stop using drugs and get my child back. She responded, "Is that all you want?" I didn't really know what she meant. I just knew that I only weighed a little over one hundred pounds and was too hungry and tried to answer any of her damn questions. I just wanted some food and a bed and not necessarily in that order.

New Life was just what its name implied. I gained a lot of knowledge about what I had been dealing with for most of my life through identity and shared experiences with other women, and I would hear about that disease called addiction again, and I began to gain a little bit of acceptance, thinking maybe I was an addict. Well, it wasn't as simple as it sounded. I stayed in New Life for a full year, learning a lot about what my problem was and listening to Emma, who loved me even when I was in a bad mood and showed me what recovery looked like in its rawest form. She was definitely a survivor, and I learned to respect her. She would share with me her experiences in active addiction. I found that she had a really hard road, much harder than I had, but she had found a way to forgive and to gain some gratitude through her recovery process. She would often tell me that I had to forgive others and myself because if I didn't, I would keep struggling. "Forgiveness is for you, not for the other person. It frees you," Emma would say.

I would hear Emma, but I just couldn't understand how I could forgive myself for abandoning my daughter, not to mention all the bad things I had done in the streets to get high. And there was no way I could forgive my uncle for what he did to me. Instead, I wanted to hate him forever and to kill them both one day—at least that's what I told myself.

I was in New Life when the nightmares started as I would wake up in a cold sweat shaking and afraid. I shared the unclear dreams with my counselor Emma, and she suggested psychotherapy. In therapy was where the memories started to surface—all the memories of my stepdad's brother coming into the girls' room in the green house. I remember him lying on top of me and touching me in places that made me feel weird. I also remember feeling afraid afterward when he would tell me not to tell anyone because if I did, I would be in trouble. He would say, "*This is our secret!*" I realized that I had been stuffing my feelings for most of my life, and I also realized how much pain I was really in after being clean for many months. I also had so many unidentifiable feelings, and my therapist began to explain to me that I had been using because I didn't want to feel anything at all. She said that I had been stuffing my feelings for so long and pushed memories so far down that it would take years for all of them to surface. My therapist called it repressed memories. As memories began to surface, all the unanswered questions started to flood my mind, leaving me physically sick and mentally depressed.

After about three months in therapy, she suggested that it was time to tell my momma about the sexual molestation. I felt like I had been accomplishing something until that point, and now I felt like a frog was in my throat, and I couldn't seem to swallow anymore! I was a twelve-year-old in a thirty-year-old body and scared all over again. All those feelings overwhelmed me, and once again, I was ashamed of myself. I began to hyperventilate and could not breathe. These things had never come out of my mouth until then, sitting in front of this stranger and telling her all my secrets that no one else knew. I had thought I could trust her, but now she was telling me to my face to repeat my secrets to the woman who hadn't protected me in the first place.

After the last therapy session, I finally got some courage and took the therapist's suggestion to write a letter because I definitely couldn't speak it out loud again, and Emma said it had to be done in order to free myself. I was still in New Life and had been there for almost a year. My daughter was in Chattanooga with my mom and my sister, and I couldn't wait to see her because I missed her so much, but I knew that this was the best way and that she was safe with them. That was the one thing I was sure of. They loved her so much probably as much as I did.

My daughter had been born on my mom's birthday, and just that fact alone assured me that she was going to be protected even if they had to take her from me for good. I can remember thinking about how I was going to tell them that I knew I had been so disappointing to them to this point, and I had mixed feelings about telling my secrets, but surely they would understand and realize that's why I had been using all these years and that I wasn't just a bad seed. They would know that I once had a heart that had been ripped apart by monsters whose names I couldn't even speak at this point. I hadn't realized the amount of pain I was really in, and because of this, I had been using a substance, trying to change the way I felt since I was twelve years old to cover up the pain, my shame, and my guilt.

It was suggested that I write a letter and send it to Momma, and I don't know why, but I was so afraid of telling her, so I wrote the letter to my sister Bria. She had always stood up for me, and I could tell that she knew that I was a good person, and I knew that she loved me even though I got on her last nerve sometimes. I knew she still loved me. She was more like a parent to me for so many years that I just felt closer to her, so after writing the hardest letter I had ever written, I sent it to my sister, and after the letter was out of my hands, I felt a sense of relief. I'm not really sure what I was actually waiting for; however, I expected some kind of response from my sister because besides my grandma, I knew that she was the other person that really cared for me, so I waited patiently for a response.

New Life was a different kind of treatment center, and although we went to church, religion was not forced on us. In fact, the church we attended was more like a women's group called Lift. We met in a group with other women and talked about our lives—how we had become addicted to drugs and how we could help one another recover. We also learned many new coping skills in regards to everyday living, such as parenting, anger management, and how to forgive others and ourselves. I met some amazing women and began right away to feel like I had a new family of sisterhood.

I had not known that so many women had been molested, abused, or abandoned in childhood, and as a result, they were using drugs, which had caused many other family issues. Some of them had been given up for adoption, and one particular woman had been discarded as trash and put in the dumpster by her own momma when she was a newborn. The stories varied, and many of them were more horrific than mine. I was in awe of their tragic lives, and this made me really mad with God. How could He allow this? He is supposed to be loving and all-powerful! How could He allow children to be treated this way? How could He care about women when He would allow daughters to be tormented? I was done with Him completely! I decided that I would never again pray to a God like this, and I didn't trust Him!

Many women came and went from New Life during that year I spent there. Many relapsed and never came back, but I was determined to stay clean because I wanted my daughter back with me, so at this point I was willing to do whatever I had to do.

Mister would come and pick me up at the bus stop because it was against the rules for any male besides our husbands to pick us up, nor was he allowed on visit day because I had shared with Emma that he sold drugs, and even though he never gave me any, I had to keep it real—he was the dope man. I was telling one secret after another, and it felt good to tell the truth about my life—the good, the bad, and the ugly—although I had not fully decided to let go of everything in my life especially not Mister. I was willing to give up the drugs! I didn't realize at the time that shooting moves, as the ladies in treatment called breaking the rules, was not conducive to my recovery, and when I would get caught doing something I wasn't supposed to be doing, Emma would often say, "You gotta change everything, girl! You can't do half-assed recovery!"

Mister would take me shopping, feed me, and drop me back off to New Life, but there were times that he would just take me to a cheap motel and give me a few dollars and drop me back off at that same bus stop, leaving me feeling like a cheap whore that had just turned a cheap trick. I knew that he had found new interest, and I was hurt but trying to hold on to him, but I could see it in his face every time he picked me up, but I still had hope. I hoped that once I completed this program, we could be a couple again and maybe get married because I could not envision my life without him, so I held on no matter how many times my feelings were hurt by him. We had talked about marriage a few times in the past, but I was too sick to marry anybody, and he was living at home with his momma and didn't even have a real job. Hustling was his way of life, but even so, I had fantasized about our wedding, our house, and our first child together.

I graduated from New Life with a year clean and had built up some self-confidence. I had been to therapy and was feeling good about myself and completed a training program in computer technology, so I felt as though I was ready to work and to live my life outside of New Life. I had some tools and some friends that really liked me, and I felt different and surer of myself. I was ready for my daughter to come home to me right away, but first I had to find a place to live of my own. See, Mister was not waiting for me with a house, nor was he ready for the new me. As a matter of fact, I don't think he liked the new me at all. I think he had a soft spot in his heart for me still and loved me dearly, but he had given up and found other interests, and he was still dealing drugs, which I hoped that he would give that lifestyle up for me, but his business was doing extremely well, and he had no plans on stopping for me.

Mister was looking good and smelling good, and the money was flooding his pockets, but I still didn't realize at this point that he was as much of an addict as I was. He was addicted to the lifestyle, and that was just as crucial as my drug addiction, but he didn't feel the need to go to treatment because his life was unmanageable because he didn't have the consequences I had—such as homelessness, helplessness, or hopelessness—and he worked for himself, so he hadn't lost many jobs, and his relationships with his family were still good. He was blinded to the fact that the enemy had him by the throat and that he was caught up in the life just as I was, so just because I was trying to get better and make a change in my life, his attitude was his problem, not mine. Mister was a fool with his money, destroying lives one at a time the same way my life had been destroyed. But he was the guy that carried that pager on his hip 24/7, waiting for that next call, that next run, and that next high.

My letter had been gone for more than six months as I waited patiently for the response from my sister. Maybe the letter had gotten lost in the mail, or maybe my sister was so distraught that it would take her a while to respond, or maybe someone else had gotten it, read it, and discarded it, or maybe it was true when my uncle said as he was raping me that he had done the same thing to my sister, and maybe my letter had brought out those feelings that she had stuffed in her own bag. I just wasn't sure, but I was hoping to hear her voice on the phone, telling me how sorry she was for all my trauma and for all the years that I had been afraid to tell anyone and all the years that they hadn't understood why I was using, but nothing yet! I was starting to feel sad and a bit hurt by the lack of response, but still I waited.

IN TRANSITION

I had been clean a little over a year and living in the transitional housing with two of my New Life sisters that the church had provided for us. I was still attending Lift Women's Resource Center, and the ladies at the church were so nice to us. They were always willing to help us with whatever we needed whenever we needed it. I didn't have any clothes when I came to New Life except one bag containing a few things that Mister had bought me at the local Kmart before dropping me off a year earlier, but now I had lots of clothes and even a place to live that I shared with two other ladies, Renae and Tesa, that I had met at New Life.

Tesa and Renae were total opposites from each other. The only thing they had in common was the addiction. Renae was a Detroit veteran, born and raised in the D from an affluent upper-class family. She had adopted the street life young due to her own defiance, and she was a hustler to her soul, and she knew how to make money and use it for whatever she wanted. She was a mom of four children and had lost them all due to her bit in the penitentiary due to her street activities. She still had her pager when she came to New Life and was fire hot when her counselor Gena took it from her. She was facing life in prison and was still going to court for the outcome. Honestly, I think she came to treatment just to escape the wrath of the court system. Ty, her baby daddy, would pick her up at the bust stop as well, just like Mister was picking me up. They were like two peas in a pod with a love-hate relationship pretty much like the one I had with Mister except she had had two babies by him. Yeah, she broke the street code!

Tesa or T-Bone, as we called her, was a Caucasian girl from North Carolina. She had two sons from a previous marriage and had been estranged from her family because of her many relationships with black men as well as her drug addiction. Trust me when I say that Tesa was not your ordinary country white girl. She talked black, walked black, loved black men, and had all black friends! She stayed in New Life for two years, and when it was time for her to leave, she cried like a first-grader being dropped off at school for the first time. She had come into New Life running from the police because she had witnessed the murder of a black man that she was dating. The police had brutally beaten him to death in front of her, and she had testified against them, and as a result, the two policemen were both in prison. During their trial, they had tried to kill her and on one occasion beat her and left her naked in a dumpster to die. Their attempts were obviously unsuccessful because here she was years later in the church house with Renae and me. At the time we didn't know anything about her court case and that she had a tag on her head until I saw her picture on the news. It was being reported that the officers were up for parole. I wasn't the only one who had secrets! She had kept this one to herself, living in close quarters with two other women, and had never said a word.

At the next Lift women's meeting after Renae and I found out that we were living with a woman on the run, Renae requested that she be put out of the house, stating, "I want her out of the house. We have kids that visit, and I don't want my kids life in danger because of her." Renae had recently gotten visitation rights to see her kids on the weekend, and she didn't want anything to happen to cause her to go back to prison or to get her rights suspended for good.

Unbeknownst to us, the pastor knew about it already, and she told us to trust God and that He would not let anything happen to us. She oftentimes used the scriptures to soothe us, saying, "*The Lord is good, a stronghold in the day of trouble, and He knows those who trust in Him.*"

I glanced over at Renae, and she had a look on her face that said, "*I'm gonna take care of this one. God don't have to worry about it!*" She was so mad at Tesa that she called Big Papa. See, before New Life, that's what she did, make a phone call to her baby daddy Ty—calling him Big Papa—when she needed him to handle a situation, and he sent his boys to deal with whatever and however! And at this point things hadn't changed too much. I was a little frightened that the police would find Tesa and hurt us all, but I didn't want Renae or Big Papa to hurt her, so I didn't know what to do or how to feel.

Pastor Aubrey was one of the founders of Lift that we had met while still at New Life, and we identified with her more than with the other ladies that ran the program at Lift because she was an ex-drug addict as well, but she called it healed, not recovery, and she didn't attend the twelve-step program that we were attending. God had delivered her in a motel bathroom, and she hadn't used since. She was so meek and humbled, and when she walked into a room, you could barely hear her coming. Her footsteps were soft, and she spoke softly. I never saw her mad, not once. She walked in love, and when she said she loved us, I knew it was real. I would often think that if she was God, nothing bad would ever happen.

I wanted to be like her. I wanted to be healed just like she had been, and I couldn't understand why God would heal her and not me. I was in recovery, but I didn't feel healed, and even though I had been clean for over a year, I still felt afraid and desperate. I wanted to hurry up and get my own place, and I wanted my daughter back right now—today! I wanted the house, the car, and I even wanted Mister to stop selling drugs and get a job so he could marry me and make me feel good about what I had accomplished. Maybe my thinking was the problem. Maybe healed wasn't a feeling but more of a fact and more of a walk like when Pastor Aubrey walked into a room, and maybe healed was more of a belief system that made it real.

It was fall, and my baby had been home with me for a few months. We finally had our own place again, and I was so excited that she was home! I was working at Technicolor in the human resources department. God had done it again—blessed me beyond measure—and I had more than enough to pay every bill that came into my house but had no clue of how to manage my money, and I didn't realize how irresponsible I had been with my finances until I got clean. See, there weren't any money-managing meetings in our home when I was growing up, and I had dropped out of school in the tenth grade, so if there were any finance classes going on in school, I missed them.

I was still in my relationship with Mister, but it seemed as though he didn't like me anymore, and I couldn't wrap my mind around the fact that the more changes I made to better myself, the more our relationship seemed to get worse, not better, and setting boundaries with him would exhalate or fighting. I had a job and was trying to practice a new kind of normal, attempting to gain some peace and serenity in my home, and I had even suggested on more than one occasion that Mister should use the money he was hustling for to go back to school and better himself as well, but he would get very offended by my suggestions, saying things like, *"Now you think you better than me! And I don't have a problem. You do!"* I got so tired of fighting him that I began to date other guys, at least meet other guys and explore my options, but Mister would show up at my house with threats of violence! On one occasion, I even got a phone call from a guy after a date that I thought had gone really well, saying, *"This is too much drama for me! I just can't be involved with this kind of thing! Call me when you get rid of this dude!"*

I couldn't believe how this guy was threatening all my dates, and I had found condoms in his car, had found phone numbers in his pants when I washed his clothes, and had even found out that he had an apartment of his own when I thought he was still living with his momma. The nerve of this guy as I was trying to make better choices for my life at the same time. It was kind of touching that he didn't want to let me go and that he loved enough to fight for me. Because of my own sick thinking, I still couldn't see how toxic our relationship was, and I still wanted so badly for him to change for me, so I couldn't give up on him. Besides, he didn't give up on me, and for that alone I felt as though I owed him a lot. Mister had been there for me through some terrible stuff, so how could he now be treating me this way? I was clean now and ready to be his wife as we had talked about when I was in active addiction, and I had held on to some of the things he had once said to me. I believed that once I stopped using the drugs and all the other behavior that came along with using that we would be okay. I had dreamed of the house that we would share together and our son that we would have. I had even picked out names for our baby boy. Even after the many abortions, I had I still had hopes of having a baby for him. I wanted more for us, and I had gotten clean for this, but the problem was that the plans were mine, not his—another fantasy that I had created, one that was mine and mine alone!

I had been clean for more than two years with still no word, no response about the letter that I had sent to my sister, so I decided to call her. She wasn't surprised at all when I asked her if she had received the letter that I sent. She said, "Yes, but I didn't respond because I just figured you was high when you wrote it." I didn't know how to feel about the fact that my sister thought that I would lie about something so serious, something that took me more than twenty-five years to tell her, something so painful and disgraceful that I had held inside for so long in order to save my family's life! My uncle had said he would kill them if I told, and I didn't want them to die. He said he had done the same thing to her and that she hadn't told either. When I was sixteen, it was disclosed that he had been raping my cousin Lea for many years, and nothing was done about it, so why would I tell? But now I was in recovery and in therapy, and it was suggested that I write this letter, by far the hardest thing I had ever done. My therapist suggested that I tell my secrets, and now here I was hurt again on the phone defending myself with the truth.

My sister called me back with my mom and auntie on the phone after she had told them what I had said in my letter. My auntie defended herself and her ex-husband and calling me a liar in so many words. I don't remember her exact words, but I do remember the silence from my momma—no words! No "Baby, I'm so sorry this happened to you," no defending me as Auntie was defending her child-molesting ex-husband! When I hung up the phone, I felt like I was twelve years old all over again. I crawled up into a fetal position while experiencing a new feeling, and I didn't even know what to call it. All I knew was that I felt like a knife was in my gut, and I couldn't pull it out, so I left that knife right there digging into my gut and shoved it into my bag along with the guilt, shame, embarrassment, degradation, isolation, distrust, hurt, and all the other new and old feelings and threw it over my back and kept it moving. I was the bag lady, and I had been trying to empty my bag, but instead, I had to make room for yet another feeling. I stopped attending church as often, and my meeting attendance would soon be nonexistent, and all those feelings of worthlessness would begin to flood my mind, and I decided that day that I wasn't going to tell anybody anything else as I allowed the short-term freedom that I had experienced to fade away.

Renae would call and ask me if I was going to church or a meeting, but I would make excuses of why I couldn't go, and sometimes I would just not answer the phone at all. I wasn't willing to talk about my feelings anymore to anybody, and I wasn't willing to surrender anymore! I would only be laughed at or called a liar. Maybe I *was* lying, and maybe all those things were a figment of my imagination, just like the wedding I had planned for Mister and me. Maybe I had dreamt up the molestation just to have an excuse for my addiction to drugs and all my other bad behavior. Maybe I was just a bad seed and belonged to the devil and was just afraid to admit it. Maybe God didn't really love me like He loved Pastor Aubrey and Renae. Maybe I could just live my life like I wanted to! To hell with what other people thought!

One thing for sure—I had my man no matter how toxic the relationship was, and I still knew how to manipulate and con to get what I wanted from *any* man. My attitude had not changed much. I didn't really have much new information, and although I was clean, I didn't realize that the recovery process was about the renewing of the mind, and I hadn't done much of that except going to the meetings, sharing my drama, and listening to others share the same, repeating my sickness over and over again, saying, "I am an addict," identifying myself as a sick person.

I would go to church on Sunday and say, "Praise God. I'm not where I want to be, but I am not where I used to be!" Those were the facts but not the complete truth. Instead, the truth was that I wanted to read the Bible and the NA book, and I wanted to change my thoughts with words as the pastor would say, and I wanted to be happy and have a good life, but I still had a lot of expectations of myself and others; and when I was disappointed or experienced a bad feeling, I would shut down and only pretend to be good. I wasn't just the bag lady. I was Ms. Feel Good by whatever means necessary, and I still didn't have the tools to deal with my feelings and emotions. Instead, I followed my feelings around as if they had complete control over me, and I acted accordingly. I allowed my feelings to drag me around by my hair, and when one feeling used me up, I shoved it back into my bag and pulled out another one.

I was only willing to do the easy part of anything, and although I was in a twelve-step program, I still didn't follow all the rules, like getting a sponsor or doing step work, changing people, places, and things, and staying clean no matter what happens. All these things sounded really good in the beginning, but I still didn't trust anyone, and those thoughts of low self-worth and low self-esteem, not to mention my fear of never having what I needed, were still alive in me, and I didn't know how to get rid of them. I was still operating from a place of self-effort, and I sure wasn't trying to meet anyone else's expectations. Hell, I was having a hard-enough time trying to meet my own!

The fact that being clean does not equal recovery was definitely an important part I had missed in the twelve-step meetings, and there was so much more to this recovery thing than I had realized, and at this point, I wasn't sure if I was up for the challenge. My repeated attempts at treatment had become insane and a bit tiresome, and I just didn't want to do any of it anymore, but every time I looked at my baby and those pretty big brown eyes, I knew she loved me, and I loved her so much that my heart would ache to think about leaving her, so I would pull a little bit of courage from the pit of my tired being and push on through another day.

I would often say that the world was ugly, and that was how I saw it because it just felt like a struggle for me all the time, but I wore it well so that no one knew I was scared to death of what the next day would bring. If I had any experience at all about living, it was keeping secrets and stuffing my feelings. I had not cried in so long that I didn't think I even had tears. I was sick, and I just didn't know how to get well. I was now in total survival mode, and those bills were going to get paid, and we were going to eat no matter what!

UNMANAGEABILITY

My life became unmanageable again. I was not going to any meetings, and I was going to church every now and then, and even though I had lived alone for some time now, I still didn't know how to pay bills or live on a budget, which I desperately needed to be doing. Instead, my way of paying bills was just to pay them whenever I could, and when I found myself overwhelmed, I would just stop paying them at all. Mister was not helping much anymore. He was in the street more than he had ever been, and it was obvious to me that he was cheating when he wouldn't answer my phone calls many nights and would stand me up like it was nothing, and when he came by for the night, I would search his pockets and his phone while he was asleep to see if there was evidence. I was so obsessed with this relationship that I didn't realize that all I had to do was end it, stop waiting up for him at night, and stop looking for something that was clearly never going to happen; but I was lonely, scared, and hurt, and I wanted to be happy, and I didn't know how to be without Mister! I could hear Emma saying, "Girl, you gotta change everything," but I felt stuck and in love with a man that could not give me what I needed not because he didn't try but because he didn't have what I needed. In my twelve-step meetings, it was often said, *"Let go and let God!"* but I didn't know how to let go. All I knew was how to hold on, and to let God would mean that I would have to let go of my fear, and I didn't know how to do that either.

I didn't realize that the disease of addiction was not just about using drugs. Instead, it was more about my thinking and my actions, and the fact that I wasn't working any program didn't help because the obsession and compulsion was really what I needed help with. I needed to learn how to live with my own feelings without allowing them to control me. I needed to accept the things that I could not control, which were very little outside of my own being. As long as I could remember, I had been uncomfortable in my own skin and so afraid to be alone, and therefore, I would become addicted to something or even someone to change the way I felt about myself and to keep me from focusing on my fear. Instead of dealing with my feelings in a healthy way, I used Mister to keep me distracted, and I was not letting him go even if it meant to the death of me. I would find out real soon that the disease of addiction was an enemy of life, not my opponent, and if I had only learned how to love myself in a healthy way by dealing with those things that were destroying my peace of mind instead of trying to change a man that I clearly had no power over, I could have heard the bells going off saying, "Surrender, the fight's over."

Mister was not my savior. He was not faithful to me, and he was not my daughter's real father, but he loved us the best he could with what he had. He didn't know how to be in love or to be all that I needed. The truth was that Mister was a drug dealer, and the streets took priority even over me, and he was just as sick as I was, and we were both operating with some misinformation. He did what he needed to do to feel like he was somebody special and maybe to fill that hole inside of him with whatever worked. He needed more women than he could handle, and he needed to lie and cheat, just like I needed the drugs to change the way I felt about myself to fill the big hole in my gut and to replace the lack of self-love in me.

I needed something bigger than he was, something more powerful than he could ever be, and I needed to surrender my entire life to that power. I needed to let someone else take the wheel because I was driving my vehicle right to the graveyard, and I couldn't find the brakes! I didn't know that the enemy was still ruling my life, and that even though the drugs were gone, I was still using all that stuff that I had tucked away in my bag to rationalize my outrageous sort of nonsense. Therefore, my behavior mimicked active addiction, and it would only get worse, and I would soon reap the benefits of my unwillingness to change completely.

REALITY CHECK

In 2000, I experienced a life-threatening event. It was the Christmas season, and Mister and I were decorating the Christmas tree. I had been to the doctor earlier that day and had been given a prescription for a medicine called Bactrim to treat a bladder infection. I remember getting a call from the pharmacy that my prescription was ready for pickup, so Mister ran out to pick up the prescription. A few minutes later, he dropped off the bag from the drugstore, saying, "Babe, I need to run off. I got business." He wouldn't participate long in something as simple as decorating a Christmas tree, and I knew I should have kept him busy while I had him, but I was used to doing things without him anyway, so I finished up the tree and took my medicine as prescribed.

Soon after taking the dose, I felt very tired and disoriented with chills as my entire body started hurting. I thought maybe I was catching a cold or the flu, so I called Mister, asked him to bring me some over-the-counter cold meds, and dozed off to sleep. Within a few hours, I was bleeding uncontrollably from every orifice in my body! I was so weak that I could hardly stand, and when I did stand, blood was pouring out of me like water running from a faucet. Mister insisted on taking me to the hospital and carried me to the car. The doctors said that I wouldn't have made it through the night because I was literally bleeding to death internally. I had been in some situations that could have killed me, not to mention all the street drugs I had put into my body that I survived, but death was something I had not anticipated while clean, especially from a legal prescription.

I lay in that hospital for almost two weeks with tubes running through my body and someone else's blood pumping into my veins to keep me alive—the blood of a stranger, someone who had never laid eyes on me, someone who did not have a clue that they would be giving blood for someone like me, a drug addict. A stranger who didn't care who got the blood had given it to me because they cared for human life. Talk about gratitude! There was some good in this world. Someone actually cared about me, and it didn't matter at that point who it was. It was a stranger who had showed unconditional love by giving his or her blood to help save a life, and the fact that I had almost died was horrific, but the fact that someone gave me there blood was more than amazing. It was beholden.

Not long after my hospital stay, Mister bought me the second engagement ring and asked me to marry him, and of course, I said yes! I had sold the first ring in active addiction, and I was so excited that he loved me enough to propose again. Well, the excitement didn't last long because a couple of months later, I found out that Mister was cheating again, but this was different. It wasn't just with some random chick. He was in a full-fledged relationship and had been for almost two years. I was devastated when the girl on the other end of the phone said that she was engaged to be married to the same man I was engaged to, my man. All those feelings of rejection came back again! All the "I love you "and "Will you marry me?" had just punched me in the face, and I started using again, and I fell hard!

I had heard in the twelve-step program that the disease of addiction was progressive and that it would get worse every time. This time it got so bad that I was stealing from my job again to support my habit, not just any job but a job that I had worked really hard to get and I really did like. I had even gotten a promotion, and every day that I went into the office, I felt nervous and guilty. I had fought for my clean time, and I didn't want to lose my baby again, so I decided to go back into a short-term rehab just to clear my mind and to get back on track. At least that's what I told myself, so I took off work on short-term medical leave, which seemed to be my best option.

I was out of rehab and had moved into another place that my girlfriend Angel had helped me get into. I attended a church service with her one evening, and a few days later, she called me to tell me that this pastor wanted to speak to me, saying that her words were for my ears only. I was a little reluctant to respond because I didn't mind church, but I still wasn't good with the God thing, and I didn't want anyone telling me about what God could do, so I responded with little concern, "Okay," but Angel would not let it go. She insisted that I called this pastor, so finally I did, and she told me that I was in a dangerous relationship but could not let it go in my own strength. She said that there were things that needed to be revealed to me in order for me to let it go, and she gave me a prayer request for God and told me to only say it when I was ready to know the truth. The pastor said to me that "God is your protector and your source, not man." It took me a while, but when I said the prayer, quickly I began to see things so clearly that I didn't have to look anymore. I was having outer-body experiences, and I could see things such as names and phone numbers of the many women that Mister had been with, and I also found out that he was addicted to porn.

THE RUNNING CONTINUES

I was clean again, and nothing was going to get in my way! I felt as though my relationship was a stumbling block, and the relationship with myself had been nonexistent, so it was time for me to focus on me and my child completely. I packed up and moved to Atlanta, Georgia, but it didn't dawn on me that I had been running most of my life, and this time was not much different. See, I was taught early on how to run but not how to stand in my own truth, so I believed that by changing my environment, my life would ultimately change. I had made many attempts to change my life in my own ability. I had left Detroit so many times in active addiction that I had lost count. I didn't know what else to do, and it just made sense at the time. But I would soon find out that it wasn't as much about changing my environment as it was about changing my thinking. I was not only running from me. I was also running from God, but how was I to trust Him when He was a man? At least that's what I thought, and He had allowed a lot things to happen to me, and I certainly didn't know *how* to change me. Hell, I didn't even know who I was! I had spent most of my childhood wishing I was someone else and many times pretending to be somewhere else, and as the years went by, I had combined all those people into one person, and that was who I thought Kiva was. It was just too painful to allow that scared, hurt little girl to come out, so she had kept quiet as I continued to abuse her one day at a time, one drug at a time, one city at a time, and one man at a time, using all those things in an attempt to change the way I felt.

After a couple few years in Atlanta, Mister asked me if he could come visit me, and I agreed because I still loved him, and I really did miss him. After a couple of visits, we decided that he would pack up his bags and move to Atlanta, at least I decided because his plans was never really clear. I was happy, but something else was happening in me, and I couldn't put my finger on it, but I knew deep down it wasn't a good idea. Mister said that he would try to get a job, and he did make attempts to search, but he wasn't finding any offers to compare to the money that he was making in the streets of Detroit, and when he would complain about it, I would remind him that he didn't have any work experience, and maybe if he could just take anything and be patient, the money would come. But his plans to travel back and forth to Detroit to make money was making me very uncomfortable, and the atmosphere in my home that I had built with my daughter began to change.

    I am a dreamer, and I believe that God has always revealed things to me in my dreams because I see things that many times comes to pass. In this dream, I would wake up go into the bathroom, and there it was, a black snake hanging on my curtain rod looking at me. I believe it was confirmation that I had opened my door up once again to the enemy. As I looked into the eyes of this snake, I could hear a voice saying, "Resist the enemy and he will flee!" I had to give the man that I depended on for my emotional support, my best friend, and my future husband an ultimatum that he would need to be in Atlanta full-time and get a real job or leave for good. The next day, I came home from work to packed bags sitting at the door. I gave him an ultimatum, and he did not choose me, and although I knew it was the best thing for both of us, it didn't stop the pain I felt from him leaving. I knew it was over, and I didn't want it to be. Instead, I wanted him to choose me and my daughter, but he made the choice that was best for him. As he walked out the door, a piece of me went with him. The codependent part of me left right along with him, and I felt like my heart had been ripped out from my chest. I couldn't stick the pain of losing Mister in my bag. It was too big, and besides, my bag was already overloaded. I had spent very little time unpacking. Instead, most of my time spent was trying to keep my man and take care of my daughter. I held on to the little recovery that I had for as long as I could, but as usual, I relapsed again, and it was worse than ever.

I was losing everything I had again. I was months behind in car payments, and I had lost my job at the nursing home because I couldn't use drugs and function to my full capacity, so we were facing eviction, and I was tired of trying to live. I was using every day and night. I was sick mentally, physically, and emotionally, so what was there left to do? I could either go on as best I could to the bitter end—jails, institutions, or death—or I could find a new way to live. But I didn't know *how* to find a new way to live. I had been trying for so long that I had no more ideas. I had been in more than eight treatment facilities, had been to jail four or five times, and had failed in religion. My family had exhausted all attempts to save me, and they were pretty much done at this point. I was not going to be a drug addict anymore, and I was not going to stay around and worry my family anymore, so at this point I felt nothing but suicidal.

It was Christmas, and I was in Jackson, Tennessee, at someone's house whom I didn't even know, using drugs and all sorts of other things, at a low that I couldn't even imagine taking myself to. I was sitting on a bed with my head hung down, sick and tired, and wondering again how I had gotten to this point. I was thinking about my daughter and how I could have done this to her again and wanted so badly to call her, but I didn't want to upset her. After all, what would I even say at this point? My heart was broken, and I could only imagine what she was thinking. I was numb inside, and all my emotions were numb as well.

My auntie called a recovering addict that I had met in my twelve-step program, asking him to look for me, and when he found me at this known drug house, he demanded that I leave with him and even called the police to get me out of this known drug house. There was always someone in my life that cared more about me than I cared about myself. The drugs had taken my soul, and I was caught up in the grips of this horrific disease again, and even though I knew that it was wrong, I just wanted to keep getting high to numb the pain I felt every time my high wore off. But after a couple of visits from my guy friend knocking on the door, I was asked to leave, so I left with him. My guy friend had over twenty years clean and was still attending twelve-step meetings and had been a support for me in the past, and even though I knew he wanted more, we only had a platonic relationship. On the ride to his house, he criticized me about using and began to get really angry because of my lack of response. He then pulled the car over in a dark wooded area and pulled out his gun and stuck it in my face, saying, *"If you wanna die, let me help you. I'll kill you right here right now*!" I didn't say a word as my heartbeat was too faint and my breath too shallow to respond, not to mention that I couldn't begin to wrap my mind around what was happening. I had been using for weeks, and I was just too weak to think about defending myself, and I was terrified and thinking that he was going to kill me, but at the same time, I didn't really care if he killed me or not because I was tired of trying to live anyway! But he put the gun away and drove me to his house.

I was eating and sleeping well for a few days, but I knew I couldn't stay there for good. I tried to go to meetings, but I was so ashamed and embarrassed that I couldn't do much sharing or listening for that matter. I missed my family, and I knew that they missed me as well, but at this point I knew they were just plain tired of me and all the drama that came along with my using. I was at such a low place, but I decided that I would try once again, so I called a few treatment facilities in Atlanta because I knew I needed to leave this my friend's house, but I wasn't strong enough to be alone, and although I had been in many rehabs, I was willing to try again.

I shared with my guy friend that I wanted to go into rehab as he was very encouraging and seemed to be on board with my decision. However, a few days later, he came home from work with a beer and offered it to me, saying, "I know you want to use, so I got you some beer." I was floored! Here we go again. This brother is crazy! First, he stuck a gun in my face and now a beer! What the heck was going on here? This brother was in recovery. He came and rescued me. He brought the police, and he even apologized for sticking that gun in my face, saying that he just wanted me to see the reality of active addiction, and although I still wanted to use, I rejected the beer, thinking maybe this was his test to see if I really wanted to stay clean.

A few days later, he gave me money and took me to buy drugs, and I did. Over and over again, day after day, he would come home from work and take me to that same house, so I used every day, and he used me for what he wanted for a couple of weeks—no more meetings, just drugs. Here I was using again and depending on a psycho recovering addict to save me, which just happened to be a man. I felt like a prisoner in this man's house as he would lock me in his house every day while he went to work, and when he came home, he would take me to get drugs. I was more than sick and tired of being sick and tired. I was sick and tired of living!

I had been using for so long that I could no longer imagine a day without drugs, and I did not want to live that way. Nothing was working anymore, not the drugs, not the men, and no matter how much I acted out on my anger and my resentments, blaming others had now gotten old, and no one was listening anyway. I was a deadbeat mom and a crackhead, and I had failed everybody, including myself, and I had been used up from childhood, and nothing and no one could help. God couldn't even help me, and if He could, He hadn't, and I was done with it all, even Him! I was sick and tired of being sick and tired, and I had no more fight in me, and I just wanted to die!

I could hear a loud voice in my ear saying, "Kill yourself. You're no good for no one!" I had failed at many attempts at working the twelve-step program, in and out of drug rehab, mental institutions, and a few overdoses. I decided that to die would be better than living in a world of chaos and confusion, and if I went to that place called hell that I had heard about all my life or wherever the bad people went, it would be better than the life I was living. I walked into the bathroom and took every pill I could find in his cabinet and swallowed them all, but just like I couldn't stay clean, I couldn't even kill myself!

After waking up regurgitating everything inside of me, I was furious and afraid all at the same time that I had survived a suicide attempt. I found myself lying on a couch trembling and in a total state of surrender, crying out for help from the pit of my soul and screaming at a God of my misunderstanding, one that I didn't trust and certainly didn't have a relationship with, but as I cried out from the pit of my soul, screaming at this God, requesting that He would either let me die or show me how to live, as a result, I was led to a powerful source called recovery, and an amazing new journey was about to begin!

Something happen that morning on that couch, and although I was so sick and too weak that I could hardly sit up, I knew that something different had just happened inside of me. I had an inner peace that I had never felt before, and although I still can't fully explain it, I knew that something miraculous happened. I don't remember calling my sister, but it was said to me that I called her right before I passed out to say goodbye to her and asked her to take care of my child. I can hear the door open, and in walked my sister and my cousin Lea, and I was so glad to see them walk into that room. I believe that the fact that they came for me was a sign from God that I was supposed to live and that my family still loved me in spite of all that I had done and the family that I was given at birth did belong to me.

I self-admitted into another rehab center in Atlanta, Georgia, where I was kept in isolation for a few days, and I slept really hard from exhaustion and fatigue. I had been in so many drug rehab centers that I pretty much knew the ropes. The only difference was that this was a center just for women and children. I didn't mind the kids so much. It was just the noise I didn't care for especially in the early morning, but it was rehab, and I was glad to be there.

I had started going to drug rehab in the early nineties, and now many years later, here I was again with so many emotions coming out at one time that I couldn't keep up. One day I would be feeling sorry for myself, and the next day I would be humbled and grateful, then the anger would come. I was mad at myself for being in this situation once again following a protocol that I knew all too well. There was nothing else to learn here. I had been given these same suggestions so many times that I knew them like the back of my hand.

I was so tired of the rehab rhetoric, and oh my God, the noise from the crying kids was starting to get overwhelming, and I was too angry to follow any more rules from anybody, so after a couple of months, I was kicked out of the center for holding a knife to a girl's throat on kitchen duty! I was given the ultimatum of leaving or going to jail, so I took the easier option and began packing my bags, and then it hit me. I didn't have anywhere to go. I was homeless because this time I had burned all my bridges, but I was not hopeless. Instead, I had started reading the Word of God and my twelve-step literature during those months, and the fear of going out into the world was no longer controlling me. I believe that I had a spiritual awakening the day God saved me from my suicide attempt, and I knew that I wasn't going to use drugs anymore, and even though I had no place to go, I had hope. After I finished packing my things, I fell to my knees and prayed my grandma's prayer. I had made up my mind that I would live on the street if I had to, but I would not use drugs no matter what, and I would never come back to another drug rehab again.

Here I was, on my last day in rehab, not because I had chosen to leave or finish the program but because of my behavior. I wasn't really angry at anyone but myself, and I was ashamed for acting out in a horrible way on kitchen duty. I had no money, nowhere to go, and no one to call, so I took a chance and called my best friend, but she turned me away, and even though that felt like a knife in my gut, I understood. I had no other option but to call my mom, but I had done her so wrong for so many years that I wouldn't have been surprised if she had not even answered the phone or had hung up at the sound of my voice. I had abandoned my daughter over and over again for her to raise, and I was a bad daughter to her, one that I knew she was ashamed of.

The ringing of the phone seemed like the slowest, loudest ringing I had ever heard. Suddenly a soft, sleepy, sweet voice said, "Hello." I hesitated, and again she said, "Hello." I had no plans of what to say, and here I was holding the phone in silence. Again she said, "Hello."

Finally I was able to muster out the word that I knew I had no right to say, but I said it anyway, "Momma, I'm out of rehab, and I don't have anywhere to go!"

Without hesitation, she said, "Okay, your sister will be there to get you."

When I hung up the phone, I was in awe, only with three words coming out of my mouth, "Thank You, God." See, I knew there was a God and that He was bigger and more powerful than any of us. I just didn't know Him personally, and I still didn't trust Him, but I knew that for my momma to allow me to come to her home or to even be speaking to me was an act of some power greater than the both of us.

A NEW WAY

My new way of life consisted of staying clean one day at a time one meeting at a time, and sometimes I had to take it one moment at a time. I would wake up and go to a twelve-step meeting. Sometimes I would attend two to three meetings a day, and that was all I did for about six months. I started looking for a job, and although my job search was a bit difficult at first, I had hope that I would find something, and I was willing to do what I needed to do. My work experience was in corporate finance, which I hadn't done since I left Detroit, I had started a cleaning business when I moved to Atlanta, and that had pretty much been my income for about four years. I had also worked as a nursing assistant, and but I got arrested in Georgia, so I couldn't work in the medical field for a while.

Here I was in Chattanooga, where all my trauma began and with the wreckage of my past staring me in the face, but I was clean, and I had hope! I didn't know what God had in store for me, but I knew that there was a God, and that was enough for the time being, so to do the next right thing and the best that I could was all that I could do. I was willing to do whatever I needed to do to stay clean and get a place of my own for my daughter and myself. Life is funny. It definitely has a way of changing our plans! There were so many things I wanted to do. As a child I dreamed of becoming a dancer and an actress, and then I went to an opera when I was just a small girl in elementary school and fell in love with the sound of the high-pitched voices and the melodies that seemed to connect to my heartbeat, so I decided I was going to be an opera singer. As the years went on and my struggles got so real, I decided that I would be a psychiatrist so that I could help people because I knew there were a lot of mental sickness in the world.

I was a dreamer, and I always wanted to make my momma proud of me, but the fear inside of me had left me paralyzed and lifeless. Most of the time I felt like a little girl was hiding inside of me and that I had to protect her, so I created a tough-girl facade, but nothing about me was tough. I was afraid of everything and everybody. I never dreamed of being a drug addict. I was just trying to stop hurting and stop being scared.

The life of a drug addict is demonic, and I would not wish it on my worst enemy. It's an evil force that moves you slowly toward a deep, dark pit that eventually pulls you in. I felt hopeless, helpless, and full of fear, and finding my way out of that pit was the hardest thing I ever had to do.

I began to question God, asking why He would allow something so destructive as addiction to even exist, and why would He allow my beginning to be so ugly? As a kid, my soul was tormented, and my body was abused. How could God be love and watch these things go on, and if He is all-knowing and could see that a huge part of my life would be ripped apart, why wouldn't He intervene? Why would He even let me have a child but not have the ability to raise her and love her like a real momma should? Why wouldn't He protect me from the horrors of active addiction, which clearly came to steal, kill, and destroy me?

I heard a pastor say once that God has given us freedom of choice, but I could not understand how a person could make a choice when they didn't have a choice to make. Instead, the ability to choose was stripped away from me at such an early age, and how could a baby have freedom of choice when pain and fear are introduced to them before they even understand what they mean?

I had about six months clean, and I was trying to understand this God that had saved me, and I was getting angrier every time I even tried reading the Bible, but I still didn't understand, and it was starting to be really hard for me to pray, and when I did pray, I felt like a pitiful soul begging for forgiveness over and over again for my many years of sin. There were times that I didn't want to talk to God at all, and when I did, I would just ask Him questions about my past and then feel guilty for questioning Him. I was still having pity parties, thinking, "Why didn't the addiction kill me from the start? Why did I have to go through the process of destruction as I started to feel powerless and empty again, and even though I was clean, I was as confused as ever?"

I knew I could no longer use any mood or mind-altering chemical to escape my feelings but there were days that I still had thoughts that maybe I could just use one of something and be all right, but I knew that was a lie, so I continued going to meetings. My feelings were surfacing and my emotions were all over the place and my tears were surfacing as I would find myself crying for no reason at all. There were still times when I didn't want to talk to my mom because in some ways I blamed her for a childhood filled with fear and pain. I still felt the hate for my father for abandoning me, and I was angry at him for dying and leaving me again with no chance of confronting him. I would talk to my sponsor because I felt like she was the only one I could really trust with my feelings, and she understood me more than anyone else. She would give me an assignment to write followed by many words of encouragement and telling me that it was okay to have feelings, but we cannot allow the feelings to have us. She would also tell me that at some point I would have to surrender the things that I could not change, and when I would tell her how I was having a hard time understanding God, she would encourage me to call God a good, orderly direction, saying that it's all about perception and that I didn't need to understand God to pray to him and that I would soon find the God of my own understanding followed by, "Just keep coming back. More will be revealed."

THE MARRIAGE

To know and trust oneself as well as having a handle on your life goal and being able and willing to make specific future plans for a life with a partner is the key to a healthy marriage.

I met my husband when I was just a little over a year clean. I was living in my own apartment, preparing for my daughter to graduate from high school. She wanted to go back to Detroit to graduate with her friends, so I agreed to make her happy for her last year in high school. I moved in with my soon-to-be husband within ninety days of meeting him as my plan hadn't been to stay with him, but I had mold issues in my apartment, and management had put me up in a hotel until the issue was resolved. However, my future husband invited me to stay with him, telling me that his mom told him that he shouldn't let me stay in a hotel. At first I was reluctant, but this man was fine, a homeowner, and a military veteran. He also had a good job and drove a very expensive car, and that was my idea of a good man, and the fact that he had already told his mom about me was definitely impressive, not to mention the fact that he treated me with the upmost kindness and respect—in the beginning.

Our fighting didn't start right away. We were in love within ninety days, at least I was. I was happy for the first time in a long time and felt like this was the man of my dreams. I hadn't been in a relationship since Mister, and I had never been in a healthy relationship or a committed one for that matter, and this just felt different. I was clean, and I thought I was ready to get married only after a year, so I was already planning the wedding in my head. I did notice a few red flags, like when I didn't answer his phone calls, he would make accusations about me cheating on him or if my phone rang too many times, he was suspicious and would question me or give me the silent treatment sometimes for days, which caused me to raise an eyebrow once or twice, but he did nice things for me, like washing my car when I was at work and would have dinner ready for me when I came home from work, not to mention the fact that he would always hug and kiss me when I came home. He was very affectionate, and I just loved it.

But soon I would notice how he would get extremely upset about the smallest things, like me not being on time for a date if we had plans or his temper going quickly from zero to ten. Or if I didn't come right home from work or wasn't home to go to bed with him at the same time at night, he would toss and turn in anger most of the night, and if I went out for a girls' night out, he would be angry and wouldn't talk to me for days at a time. I hadn't been in this type of relationship before, so I figured I could handle it, and besides, I knew he was committed to me because he came home every night, which I was not used to, so I figured I could live with the little irritating things, so I embraced all of it.

The first-time things going to the extreme was when he got upset at me for staying out overnight with my best friend. He and I had been arguing earlier that day, and I was a bit overwhelmed, so I grabbed a bag and told him that I was gone for the night. I came home the next morning to a loaded gun lying on the dinner table. I asked him why it was there, and he replied, "I was waiting up for you all night, so I cleaned my gun!" I thought, "Well, damn!" I could also see that the jealousy and control issues were starting to get a bit more intense, but still I told myself that I could handle it, so I stayed and argued and tried to figure him out. I was a bit confused by the fact that my friends made him uncomfortable, and he repeatedly would tell me that he didn't trust them—or me for that matter. I knew he was faithful, but so was I, but I still spent a lot of time defending myself, and the fights escalated.

In spite of all the drama and our differences, my plan was that we would be married in two years. I was going to have a husband by any means necessary, and I wanted him, and when I gave my husband-to-be an ultimatum and he ran out and got my ring, I wasn't sure how to feel about it, but in spite of all the fighting, I wanted this and thought I deserved a husband, and if I was going to stay with him, then he would have to marry me. I was not going to allow any man to ever use me again, so I said to him, "Marry me, or I will leave!"

I had been in my last relationship for more than sixteen years with Mister, and it was total chaos. I was addicted to drugs during most of that relationship, and when I got clean, I tried to make Mister marry me, but we never made it to the altar. I was very emotionally deprived, and I needed someone not only to love me but also to prove it. And I needed this love to come from a man because when I was a young child, my father had abandoned me and had never held me or told me that I was good enough, and although I had no respect for any man, I still thought that I needed that hole in my gut to be filled with a man's love, so with four years clean, we stood in front of a pastor with my brokenness and my husband's insecurities and said, *"I do."*

I thought things would settle down after the wedding. Although we had been fighting all the way to the altar, I still thought, probably like many women that desperately want to be married, he would change once I became his wife. My husband had experienced deception in his last marriage, and on many occasions I wasn't sure if he was talking to me or if he was still in that marriage, and being that I am very intuitive, I realized that he had not healed from that deception and was still bitter and living in resentments that had nothing to do with me, so defending myself was a total waste of time. Our conflicting personalities didn't make it any easier, so having a conversation with him could be very difficult and would usually end in an argument. Mark 3:25 says, *"If a house is divided against itself, that house cannot stand."* We tried counseling, but nothing seemed to be working. I even went to therapy without my husband, searching for a solution to a never-ending battle, and interestingly enough, I would most often times end up in a therapist chair answering questions about my past, but I wasn't there for that, the issues I had. I was there to try and figure out my husband.

I went to my meetings almost every day to talk about what I was feeling, but I just couldn't seem to share away the pain and discontentment that I felt inside. Maybe I was still trying to fix the inside with outside stuff, and at some point, I realized that the marriage was definitely outside stuff. I was afraid to leave and afraid to stay, and the spirit of fear had tormented me for so long that I didn't even realize that I had married my husband in fear. I was afraid that I would never have a husband and that no man would ever accept me, and I feared that once they found out about my past, they would run for sure, so I needed to get married really quick. I didn't know that the void inside of me was too big for any earthly man to fill and that only God could mend the wounds and fill that deep, dark hole inside of my soul. I was desperate to have someone there next to me, to hold me, and to make it all okay even at the expense of my safety, but I didn't have much self-love or any information about marriage. Only fear was what I knew! It was my best friend, and anger was my greatest weapon. These defects kept me hiding, kept me in secret, kept me in ego, and kept me sick.

The marriage happened despite our differences and all the fights and the sleepless nights, and although I didn't get the wedding I wanted, I compromised because I was desperate. We spent our honeymoon at the hotel in downtown Chattanooga, and for the most part I was happy and figured that once we were married, things would definitely get better. However; things didn't get better because we were married; as a matter of fact, I think they got worse. We were two very different people, and neither of us was trying to submit to the other, and I definitely wasn't going to submit myself to any man, so I was mean and spiteful. I was the victim, and I complained about our marriage to everybody that would listen. I whined and complained all over town.

When I would ask my husband if he was happy, he would respond by saying, *"Yes, Kiva, marriage has its ups and downs. We are going to be all right."* In spite of how I was treating him, my husband would say, *"I'm not a quitter. I'm in this for life!"* Although he had many insecurities, I knew that he loved me the best he could, and even though it was a sick kinda love, he was committed to me about as much as I was to him. I would often share my past life with him in hopes of bringing us closer together, but it would backfire on me, seemingly giving him more ammunition not to trust me. The reality of it all was that we were both self-centered, and we each had our own resentments to deal with, and neither of us was ready for marriage.

I was the bag lady, and I had no idea that I needed to completely unpack my bags before I got in any relationship with a man or married for that matter, and the fact that it took so much sacrifice to be with someone else was more than I could handle, and there was absolutely no acceptance on my part and definitely no willingness to surrender my will to any man. The truth was that I was still living in my feelings, and the disease of addiction was manifesting itself in other ways, and the twelve-step program was all I could give my full attention to, so my husband got whatever I had left, and the resentments were still as much alive in me as the day I started using many years prior. I was still trying to figure out where I was headed in life and who I was as a person because I still didn't know, and the search to find myself left little time or attention for anyone else let alone a husband, so our arguments escalated, and the fights continued. I didn't want anyone to have my husband's attention but me, and I wanted my way all the time.

We would often argue about his relationship with his daughter and how he would seemingly allow her to manipulate him and dismiss my every opinion about it. I didn't understand a father-daughter relationship because I had never experienced one myself. I wanted to understand the relationship they had, but my questions seemed offensive to him, and he would shut me out every time. I loved his kids, but I wanted him to trust me and make life decisions with me. I had been fighting for the love of my father for so long and looking for a man to fill his shoes that my relationships were all based on the fact that I didn't have my daddy and was angry about it. I admired my husband's relationship with his kids, but at the same time, I was jealous and resented him for not including me.

We were two people existing in a home together, pretending to be happy, at least he was, but I was screaming all over town to anyone who would listen to my self-pity, leaving every now and then only to return back to the same toxic environment with my insane thinking expecting different results. I was still desperate, wanting my marriage and wanting to be loved while compromising every ounce of peace that God Himself had sacrificed for me, still controlled by the spirit of fear and my distorted thoughts of what if, if only, and just one more time, so I suggested marriage counseling, and my husband agreed to go only to hear what I already knew—that the two of us should not be married. The marriage counselor even refused to counsel us together. She said that we both had our separate issues to deal with and thought it would be best if we sought counseling separately. But I was not giving up! I knew that God honored marriage and that He had changed my life for the better, and I had no doubt that He could change our marriage.

HIS WAY

I decided to pray that God would change my husband while sitting in my bubble-filled bathtub, where I would often pray, "God, please change my husband and make him see that I love him and make him love me back."

I heard the Holy Spirit speak to me, asking, "Why?"

"Why?" I responded.

Again I could hear a subtle voice saying, *"Why would I change him for you? If I change him, it will be for my glory, not yours."*

I sat in that bathtub until my skin was wrinkled because what I heard would mean that if God wasn't going to change him, then maybe I was the one that needed changing. I felt so hopeless and powerless that out of my own mouth came the words that "I would rather be using drugs than to deal with this any longer." I had tried to fix my marriage every way possible, and I had even invested in self-help books. I wanted my marriage to work because I didn't want to be alone, and the thought of another failure at anything would mean that I was a failure all over again. I had failed at so many things, and this was not going to be another failed attempt! But something was really wrong here if the thought of going back into that hell of a lifestyle that should have killed me, that nearly destroyed everything that I love and took me to a low that I would never forget, seemed better than being in this marriage. Something definitely had to change, so again I cried out, saying, "God, I can't take this anymore," and I could hear that same voice speaking to me, saying, *"Leave and take nothing!"* So after seven years of marriage, I left and didn't take anything but my clothes and my car.

I left my husband for the third time and moved to Charlotte, North Carolina, with my girlfriend Geana. I thank God for her because no matter how much I complained and whined about my marriage, she never judged me, and when I told her I couldn't take it anymore, she didn't hesitate, saying, "Girl, you can come live with me! I got your back. You know how we do!" So I packed my clothes into my car and drove to Charlotte. At the time I didn't realize that God was moving me into isolation, a place where I could hear Him clearly. I was so busy crying out that I couldn't hear the wisdom that He wanted to give me through His word. I could read, but I was so much in my self-obsession that I hadn't been able to get the information I needed in order to get clarity. I still wasn't trusting in God. Instead, I was trying to control my life all by myself and shouting out to Him when I couldn't handle it anymore, just like when I did in active addiction.

I was a runner and had been for most of my life! I would run to something or someplace instead of confronting or dealing with consequences. I've come to realize that through all the years that I have been running, I may have been running from God, not allowing Him to be the Father I so desperately needed, not allowing the Holy Spirit to minister to me and to give me wisdom. I was ignorant to God's way, and I didn't have enough patience even to *learn* His way. I only knew *my* way, and I didn't realize that I was fighting my husband in my own power, causing division in every way, and that by doing so, I was inviting the enemy into our home over and over again. I didn't know why I kept coming back. I thought it was because I wanted my marriage. I didn't realize that I didn't really want a marriage. I wanted a father to love me and speak to a place that had been tormented for so long that no human power could reach it.

My spirit was broken, and there was no way that I was going to survive in any marriage or healthy relationship until I first had one with God. I was still sick and suffering, and I was clean but still fighting. I was free but still living in bondage and living by the same spiritual principles, clean as I had been, when I was in active addiction, and even if I had married love himself, I still would not have been able to love him back. I didn't even believe that my husband married me because he wanted to. Instead, I thought that I had manipulated him to do what I wanted him to do and that sooner or later, he would realize it and change his mind especially after I told him my secrets. The enemy was still speaking to me, saying, *"He don't know who you really are!"* and *"You can't trust him. He's no different from all the other men you've been with!"* I believed that because I had allowed myself to become vulnerable to a man. He would deceive me, use my past against me, and then abandon me, so I was in constant battle to not allow this to occur.

It was still all about *my* feelings and what *I* needed, and I didn't care about what *he* needed. Besides, I'm the one that was hurt as a child and addicted to drugs because of it. Hell, I deserve whatever I want from any man—they all owe me! This was my attitude, but God began to show me that if I wanted to be married and free from the resentments that have the ability to destroy any relationship, I had to allow Him and only Him to heal me in that place of brokenness.

While in Charlotte, I began to see that my abandonment issues were still controlling my decisions, and I had been operating out of diseased thinking for so long that I didn't realize my addiction was still running my life. I didn't know anything about marriage or what it took to be someone's partner, and I didn't have any healthy examples of marriage growing up. My mom had been married a couple of times. Both of my aunts had had several husbands, and my grandparents had been separated for as long as I could remember. But this time, leaving felt different. I felt liberated, and I felt as though I could breathe for the first time in a long time, and I felt like I was having a spiritual awakening concerning the inner me, and I felt free, and I wanted this feeling to last. I didn't want to go back to chaos, so I asked my husband for a divorce, and he agreed to file.

I didn't have anyone else to look to or blame for my unmanageability, and I started to realize that I was still angry at myself for the choices I had made and that most of my decisions had been made out of desperation. I wasn't marriage ready. Instead, I was still emotionally bankrupt, and even though I wasn't using any drugs, I was still operating from a place of hurt and fear. I realized that I wasn't trusting God and was depending on my husband to take care of me physically and emotionally, and I wanted him to make me feel secure, something I had never felt, but the problem was that he was just another man doing the best he could with what he had, and I had made him my higher power—my God—by depending on him for my emotional stability, but God was there speaking into my spirit and correcting me, and I was ready to receive.

The Bible speaks about how a husband should treat his wife in Ephesians 5:25: *"Husbands, love your wives, just as Christ loved the church."* The problem was that I wasn't a wife. I was still a little girl looking for her daddy to tuck her in at night, to look under the bed and in the closet, and to assure her that she was safe. I wanted my husband to give me what I had never gotten from my father, and I wanted him to fill that hole in my gut that I just couldn't seem to get filled with anything, anybody, or anywhere.

I can recall a conversation I was having with my girlfriend Renae. She had been married and divorced by this time, and we were talking about marriage, and I can remember her asking me if I loved my husband, and I answered yes, and she replied, "You don't love your husband!" She went on to say that he was no different from all the other men I had dated. She did not sugarcoat anything for me, and she knew me better than I knew myself. I hadn't even invited her to my wedding because I knew she would have kept it real with me. And when I said to her that he's going to pay for treating me the way that he was, she looked at me with eyes that could see right through me, saying, "They all pay, baby, they all pay!" I resented her for saying that, but she knew me like nobody else did, and it was so true, and even though I resented her for being honest with me, I believe that she gave me just what I needed—the truth. I didn't need is a yes-man, someone that would just agree with me for the sake of friendship, and my girlfriend Renae was definitely not a yes-man!

WHAT'S LOVE GOT TO DO WITH IT?

He that loveth not knoweth not God; for God is love.

—1 John 4:8

Early in recovery, I received God as my Lord and Savior, but I still didn't know much about God, but I decided to take a chance on this saved thing because I saw it working in other people's lives, but I still had some issues with trusting Him completely because I was still living in my feelings, and I didn't realize that it wasn't about my feelings. Instead, it was more about facts, and the facts are that God is love and that He created me in love in spite of what my feelings told me, but I had been living by what I felt for so long that my feelings were all I could trust. I thought that God had forgotten about me and that I was so messed up that He could never love or forgive me, but I didn't know that by accepting Him as my Lord and Savior, I was receiving His love.

I had heard it many times—that God is love—in a song or in church just before the preacher said, *"If you're not saved, you going to hell!"* and "If you don't forgive other people, *God won't forgive you!"* leaving me uncertain about the choices I had made. So even though I was now considered saved, I was more afraid than ever that I still couldn't please God, and when I would leave church, I usually felt condemned. Therefore, I was still struggling with this love thing and this God thing. I would try to follow what my pastor said because I knew that some power greater than me had brought me out of active addiction and turned my life around, but I was still living in fear. The Bible says in Deuteronomy 31:8, *"Fear not, neither be dismayed, because He will not fail us or forsake us."* But my entire life had been controlled by fear and felt like I had already been forsaken and abandoned when I was just a kid, so I believed that God's love was for perfect people that went to church every Sunday and had no secrets, and that was not me.

Love had already cost me more than I could pay. People had said they loved me for many years only to abuse me, leave me, and not listen to my cry for help, so I didn't even like love from what I knew about it. I believed that love had many definitions depending on who was saying it, and when I would hear that God knows everything about us and He knows what we will go through even before we know, I would often think, "What kind of God is this? If He knows bad things are going to happen, why wouldn't He stop them? Isn't He supposed to be almighty and all-knowing?" I was still angry with God, and I didn't understand Him at all, and I still hated all men and felt entitled to whatever they had to offer. I was still the little girl that was operating out of pain, hurt, and lack of self-love, and I couldn't forgive the people that had hurt me, nor could I forgive myself for the horrific choices I had made, leaving me angry and confused.

I had been playing the blame game most of my life, and when I got clean, I wasn't just angry. I felt condemned, and I couldn't understand that if God never caused any bad, then how could He use the bad for our good? It was just all too much for my small brain to comprehend. I remember thinking that I would rather just go to hell because it seemed to be too much to please God, and no one will ever hurt me again, not even God. I wanted someone to love me, and I wanted to love someone back, but I didn't know how to give or receive love.

The truth was that I didn't really know anything about love, so I had formed my own definition, and it was terribly distorted. My sponsor told me to pray to a higher power and not to worry so much about the Bible or the church for a while and to give myself a break and just be okay with who I was instead of trying to be perfect. She would often talk about how important self-love was, which in her opinion was the best love, saying that if I learned how to love on me, I would attract love from others, and if I could only focus on the things that I could change and learn to accept the things that I could not change, gradually things in my life would change one day at a time. She would continue to reiterate that life is a process, and so is recovery.

THE SPIRIT OF FEAR

Fear not, for I am with you; be not dismayed, for I am your God.

—Isaiah 41:10 (NKJV)

It was a hot and sunny weekend in Kannapolis, North Carolina. I knew it was especially hot this particular morning because I could feel the sun shining on my face as it greeted me through my blinds coupled with the sound of my coffee pot dinging. I would usually lie silently for a few minutes, allowing my waking thoughts to pass through my mind, giving them time to slow down, as a water faucet slows to one drip at a time. Then I would grab my Bible off the side table and read a scripture. Sometimes I would just breathe and say, *"Thank you, Lord, for waking me up and allowing me another day clean."*

But this was a different kind of morning; it was the day for the story's convention at the Refuge, a local church in Kannapolis that I had begun attending since moving to North Carolina more than a year ago. I was invited to the Refuge for the Awakened service for women one Thursday night by my girlfriend Kat, and although my church home was in Atlanta, I was in a new area, so I was open to visiting local churches. Pastor Jay and all his associate ministers were amazing! I enjoyed the way they each have their own unique way of teaching the Word. Pastor Jay would break down the scriptures from the Bible, which would make it easy to understand as he explains in detail how to apply the word of God to our everyday lives. He says that trusting God and making Jesus our Lord and Savior can change our perspective and ultimately give us a more meaningful experience here on earth. I was especially excited about this convention because it was for the women, and I had been hearing about the powerful women speakers that would be coming from all over the country. So I had to get up and get going!

One of the speakers at the Awakened service shared her experience of dealing with fear and the process of overcoming what she called a demonic spirit. She said that this spirit has the ability to attach itself to us over time. The speaker said that she had asked God for deliverance, and He had revealed to her that she needed to share her testimony with other women in order to find true freedom. I for one have been tormented by fear for most of my life, but I didn't know that fear was a spirit. In fact, I've never thought much about what fear was. I've always related a spirit to a ghost, so I couldn't imagine it being attached to me. I guess it does make sense because at one point, fear had invaded my life so much that it affected my ability to rest through the night.

The speaker's message brought to mind a sermon that I had heard in the past by Kenneth Copeland. He said that *we should never go to sleep in fear. Instead, we should deal with it by reading the Word of God and declaring that the Holy Spirit is our Protector and Comforter.* I was led to Psalm 91, which is now one of my favorite scriptures in the Bible, and I read it often especially when I have a hard time sleeping. Pastor Copeland goes on to say that we will never experience an increase in our lives with the spirit of fear controlling us. I decided to start reading the scripture consistently every night before bed, and as a result, I started to experience temporary freedom from fear one night at a time. Fear is something that I had been dealing with for most of my life, and I now had some new information about this spirit, so I decided that I would not allow fear to control me anymore.

RENEWING MY MIND

I wasn't using drugs or living a toxic lifestyle any longer, but I was still unhappy and was still experiencing feelings of fear and anxiety. At one point, I felt like I was losing my mind, and I couldn't make a decision to save my life, leaving me with feelings of depression; therefore, antidepressants became my solution for several years in recovery. I would still stress out over things like money, and if I didn't have enough, I would think about stealing it or doing something disgraceful to get it, and although I wouldn't usually act on the thought, I was still left with the feelings of guilt and shame just for having the thought.

I have come to realize that renewing our minds is an absolute necessity for a new way of life because if the way we think doesn't change, there is no way that our lives will transform. It has definitely been a process for me but vital for my spiritual growth, but unfortunately for many people something traumatic or disturbing has to happen in order for the desire to change comes about. How we think could make the difference in our ability to cope and to have a prosperous life here on earth. I began educating myself with different types of literature. At first it was just step work, reading a lot of literature in my twelve-step program and also having literature study meetings with my sponsorship family, but after working the steps a couple of times, I realized that there was still something missing because my thinking was still a bit distorted, and I had very little control over my emotions still after being drug-free for years.

I began listening to my pastor teach the word of God, and I realized that this God that he was talking about was not the one I grew up with, and for once I wasn't leaving church feeling guilty and ashamed of myself; instead, I was feeling loved and forgiveness, so I wanted to learn more, and as a result, my church attendance increased, and so did my study time. I learned how to talk to God in prayer instead of begging Him for forgiveness. After all, one of the suggestions from my sponsor and the twelve-step program was to pray to a God of my understanding. I didn't stop there. I also started reading and listening to inspirational teachings, and by doing so, my thinking very slowly began to take a turn for the better. Don't misunderstand me when I say nothing happens overnight—after all, my thoughts were not shaped in one night—but I could feel something different happening each day. For example, I became more assertive and less aggressive in the way I speak to and treat others. Now the patience thing was still an issue for many years. I still wanted *what* I wanted *when* I wanted it, but I became more open-minded and started to notice that arguing over things that had no substance didn't seem to mean much anymore; therefore, I didn't need to always have the last word, and for me, not having to be right all the time took a lot of conflict and confusion out of my life.

My desire, first and foremost, is always to stay clean and have fellowship with other recovering addicts, but something about reading the Word of God started to send me in a different direction. I found by spending more time alone as opposed to being with people gave me peace of mind. Now that may seem a little selfish, but over the years, I've come to realize that spending time alone with a good book is very comforting to me and meditating, or just sitting still with my thoughts early in the morning tends to give me more clarity and insight about my day and the ability to function with a level head. I began to see my patterns of the past and how my life had really unraveled and become toxic over time. It wasn't just my past drug use. In fact, the drugs were just a symptom of an underlying issue. It was more about my thinking that had my life in shambles for many years. I started to see how unmanageability was still present in some areas of my life even though I wasn't using anymore. I always knew that I was in the wrong place doing the wrong thing when I was using drugs, but I felt so powerless and weak, and my thinking was so distorted that it would usually lead me on a cycle of insane behavior. I could hear my pastor saying, *"With all you're getting, get understanding,"* which would confirm that if I wanted my life to change, I would have to allow God to change my thinking with His word, and as result, I began to find my true identity. I began to realize that living life is more about having peace and joy and having self-love because if I could learn to love and honor myself, that same love would spill over on others! Now I understand what my mom meant when she would say that you can't love nobody if you don't love yourself.

I remember when I was struggling, trying to stay clean, and a good friend of mine, Kurt, told me to do something spiritual every day, and it would sustain me. It's funny now because it took me a long time to do it. Honestly, I didn't really understand what he meant because for a long time I got spiritual mixed up with religion, so at the time, I didn't know any better, and I was too prideful to ask him to explain it to me, so I just responded, "Okay." But today I understand that Kurt was talking about feeding my spirit man! Just like we feed our physical selves, we have to feed our spiritual selves, and that can only happen with spiritual food. There was a time when I would struggle and not really understand why my thoughts were so destructive, by reading something that pertains to a godly life not only gives me clarity, but I oftentimes also gain wisdom, knowledge, and understanding about the things that go on in my mind, and my thinking has definitely taken a turn for the better, just like Kurt said.

I started to listen more often and read books from several other faith-based ministries, such as Gloria and Kenneth Copeland and Bishop T. D. Jakes, and have not only been enlightened by the information about God but about the enemy as well. I know now that I do have a choice about the kind of life I live, and I realize that there's a spiritual war going on and have been in me for most of my life. But now I have weapons that I can use to keep Satan, Lucifer, the disease of addiction, or whatever you want to call that demon out of my life and out of my ear by using the word of God. I thank God for faith-based ministries such as World Changers Church that are willing to bless people around the world. I want to be just like them "when I grow up."

I would love to be in a position to bless a billion people before I leave this earth, and I appreciate Gloria Copeland's transparency. I heard her speak about how she and her husband were broke in the past and how prosperous they are now without any lack but not just financially. She speaks about her health and relationships being well without sickness and disease. This new information has really blessed me and given me a hunger for the word because I want my life to reflect goodness. I don't just want money. I want full prosperity, nothing broken and nothing missing, and I want to leave a legacy and a good name behind so that my daughter will be proud of me even when I'm gone. I want her to say, "My momma was amazing."

I read a book by Kellie Copeland-Kutz, *Protecting Your Family in Dangerous Times*. I was so blessed by that book, and it has given me freedom from worry in regards to my own family. I used to spend so much time worrying about my daughter, especially when she was in college. I would call her at least five times a day, and when she didn't answer the phone, I would leave multiple messages. She would call back and say, "Momma, what is it? What's wrong?" And it didn't stop there. When she got her own apartment, I still would harass her even though I knew I was getting on her nerves! I couldn't help it because I had my own abuse issues and was so afraid that something like that would happen to her. But then I read in Kellie's book, *"Because we are the righteousness of God, we can plead the blood of Jesus over our kids and our entire family. That's what we have to do and then rest in the finished works of Jesus Christ, our Lord and Savior."* When I learned that my baby would be safe and covered and that no harm could come to her if only I would plead the blood over her, I wanted in.

When I think about that, it brings tears to my eyes that Jesus loves me enough to not only protect me but my baby girl as well. I could go to sleep at night, knowing that she was safe all the way in Alabama and New York and wherever she decides to live and that nothing and no one could come near her dwelling to harm her. I can simply plead the blood over her every night, lie down, and have sweet sleep! Oh my God, who knew? I sure didn't! All this information was hidden in a book that had been written just for me. I was blind, but now I see, and I will never *not* see again. I love this new way of life and all this new information. I share these teaching with my daughter, so when she has her own family, she will know how to protect them as well, and she will never have to be filled with worry and fear.

My pastor preached a sermon about condemnation that freed me from the inside out because when I got clean, I felt that I was still condemned and thought I had done too much to be forgiven. There was no way I could even forgive myself let alone expect a perfect God to forgive me. But when I read John 3:17 (KJV), *"For God sent not his son into the world to condemn the world; but that the world through him might be saved,"* I was ecstatic! I had heard many times how Jesus had died on the cross for us, but I thought that we had to be good all the time in order for Him to love us, or He would get mad and send us to hell! It made sense to me at the time because if I had given my blood for a bunch of evil, sinful people, I would expect them to worship me all day every day, and they better not sin or else! So after reading that scripture, I started to rethink everything I had been taught about God.

When I first got saved, I was living in Detroit and still experiencing some of the same struggles, and for years I would continue to use drugs because I didn't know who I was, and I still didn't trust God or anyone else. Instead, I trusted what I knew, and I operated from my old way of thinking. The Bible tells us to trust in the Lord with all our heart and lean not unto our own understanding. At the time I was still leaning on my own understanding because I couldn't grasp that *getting* saved was an event, but *living* saved was a process. I didn't know how to let go of all my stuff, especially the years of torment, not just from the trauma that I had endured but also from my own self-inflicted abuse, and I wasn't yet faithful to anything other than what I had been operating from for most of my life, which were my feelings and my pain! I was saved but still afraid, and I held on to my survival skills and continued to operate out of the stuff I trusted just in case God didn't come through, and even though that stuff never worked for my good, it was familiar and my own personal comfort zone.

I thought that when I got saved, things like fear and resentment would magically disappear, but now I know that old stuff doesn't just go away when we get saved. There are a few things we need to do for our own personal salvation, things like reading, praying, and creating healthy relationships with other saints so they can pray for us and with us. I didn't realize at the time that my spirit was saved, but my flesh was still addicted to a lifestyle I had been living for many years, so things were still working against me, and my life kept ending up in shambles. I have come to find that Christianity is not an elbow rub or a hug in church when we say the sinner's prayer, and God was not to be played with. He had already rested in His finished works, but for me I was just beginning.

THE LITTLE GIRL

I did my work by going inside of my very being and found the solution to a very dark, confusing, and destructive path. It wasn't easy. In fact, it took time, commitment, and faith, and what I discovered was a little girl that had never been acknowledged. In fact, she was still at the bathroom sink, where she had been left many years prior, with a silent cry and a scream that could not emerge. She was never allowed to publicly exist because she was ashamed of herself, and the very thought of this frail little body being inside of me made me feel sick and sad. The little girl was twelve years old and had not spoken a word in years because the pain she had endured had left her in a silent fear, and she wasn't in any way prepared to deal with her trauma. She didn't have the confidence or the courage to confront her aggressors and was afraid to tell anyone that she was afraid, so she hid herself and only peeped out every now and then to see if it was safe to emerge, so she continued to suffer in silence. As I went deeper inside, I began to realize that the pain and fear that had my life in a seemingly debilitating state lived inside of the little girl, which would bring clarity of what I was experiencing. I also found that I could not recover my own destiny without first reaching inside to heal the little girl inside of me. I tried, but I couldn't do it on my own. I needed help not from man but from a power greater than all! I began to ask for help from the God of my understanding through prayer, and I found out that God does not waste pain. Instead, He would use my pain to deliver others.

CLEAN AND SERENE

When I got clean this last time, I recommitted my life to Christ. My desire was no longer just to stay clean, but I wanted more of a prosperous life, like I would hear the pastor in church talk about, with nothing missing and nothing broken. I wanted a husband, a home, and a better education. I was definitely open-minded and willing to do whatever it took to have a peaceful and joy-filled life. I learned that the only way I could truly heal from the inside out was to have a solid relationship with God and allow Him to expose my true identity. I found out that I had a spiritual void that could only be filled by a spiritual force and that all my attempts to stay clean and to live better had been in my own strength, leaving me frustrated and worn out. The enemy had been beating me over the head for years on end, but enough was enough! I was sick and tired of going around in circles, and I was ready to receive the promises of God that I had been reading about, and now I knew that they were available to me through the blood of Jesus, and I wanted in.

The Bible tells me in Psalm 37:4 (KJV), *"Delight thyself also in the Lord, and he shall give thee the desires of thine heart."* I want the full prosperity that the Word says we can have, and I want to know more about the abundant life. I don't ever want to live in fear again or to hold on to all the old stuff and the self-inflicted abuse that had stripped me of all my dignity. Instead, I want to know why I was created and what God's perfect plan for my life is.

I found that the more I read the Word, the more my victim mentality was leaving along with a lot of guilt and shame that had plagued me for many years. The definition of a victim is *"someone who has suffered as a result of someone else's actions or beliefs as a result of unpleasant circumstances."* I was a victim, and I owned it, and I hated every man for it. They had hurt me by touching me in places that made me feel ashamed, embarrassed, and a lot of other stuff that I had not been able to identify as a child. I was especially angry at my father for leaving me and not protecting me, and I despised God because He had let these things happen to me. I was sick and broken at an early age, and I committed many sins because of my brokenness, leaving me suicidal and homicidal. At some point, I took ownership of the abuse! It became my abuse and mine alone, but I didn't realize how the enemy had tricked me through other sick people's sin. Sick made me sick, and I received it.

I didn't know that God cared about what happened to me or loved me. At one point He was just another man, and if I didn't act right, He would punish me as well. On the other hand, I did believe He created us because that's what I was taught, so I thought that He was more like my momma, a provider, not someone to talk to. However, the Bible tells me that God was angrier about the abuse than I was. I read in Luke 17:2 (ESV) that *"it would be better for him if a millstone were hung around his neck and he were cast into the sea than that he should cause one of these little ones to sin."* Now that scripture may not mean a lot to some people, but when I looked deeper into that scripture and found that God refers to the little ones as children, I was once an innocent child, His child, so I was not a fatherless child. The fact that my daddy left me and didn't protect me does not make me less than anyone else in God's sight. He loves me and has always loved me. Even when I didn't know Him or trust Him, He still loved me.

Today I am being empowered by this new information that I find in the Word. Psalm 127:3 (NLT) says that *"children are a gift from the Lord; they are a reward from him."* I didn't know that God considered me a gift. I just knew that I was a scared little girl and that I was going to be punished for my sins, and as an adult, I was a failure that had been using for so long that there was just no hope. By reading and getting new information, I have found that many of my personal beliefs were distorted and passed down to me, either by misinformed people or by some of the experiences that I had when I was growing up.

There are several books that have encouraged me a great deal on my new journey. The blue book that I read in my recovery program said that I was not responsible for my addiction, but I *am* responsible for my recovery and that I need to be honest, open-minded, and willing to change if I want a new way of life. I definitely wanted to live differently, but I didn't know what to do in order to accomplish it. I needed help, but I couldn't find the words to ask for help. Besides, I didn't really believe that anyone *could* help me or even cared enough to want to, but at the end of a very destructive road, I was very willing, open-minded, and ready to take full responsibility.

Joyce Meyer has been a positive role on my spiritual journey. In her book *Battlefield of the Mind*, she writes, *"Our past may explain why we're suffering, but we must not use it as an excuse to stay in bondage."* I love that quote because it confirms that change is possible and that I don't have to live my life according to the things that have happened in my past. I was a prisoner of my own mind, consumed by my own guilt, and the enemy had tricked me most of my life because I didn't know any better, but today I *do* know better, and I know that I have been delivered out of bondage. Deliverance is defined as *"a rescue from bondage or danger."* In the book of Exodus, God is defined as the deliverer of Israel who rescues His people, not because they deserve to be rescued but as an expression of His mercy and love, and that statement alone qualifies me because without a shadow of a doubt, I know I don't deserve it. But when I read the Bible, I find that the grace of God is unmerited favor. Just like my pastor says, "It's not about me. It's all about God."

God loves me in spite of me and all my imperfections. We don't have to stay in bondage, and that is the good news! We can be free whenever we choose, and as Christians we have the power through Christ Jesus. The Bible says in John 10:10 (NIV), *"The thief does not come except to steal, to kill, and to destroy. I have come that they may have life and that they may have it more abundantly."* Jesus refers to Himself as the Good Shepherd and to us as the sheep, and He says that he laid down His life for the sheep. When I read the parable about the lost sheep, I saw unconditional love like never before. Luke 15:1–7 (NKJV) tells the story of a man who owned one hundred sheep, but one of the sheep was lost, so the man left his ninety-nine sheep and went to search for his one lost sheep. The Bible says that when the man found the lost sheep, *"he laid it on his shoulders and rejoiced, and when he returned home, he called together his friends and neighbors, saying, 'Come rejoice with me.'"* Imagine if, when we were lost in our sins, Jesus had said, "Well, I have many more children, so I won't worry about that one." But instead, Jesus cares for each of us equally. He doesn't operate like man does. I didn't know that He wanted me when I was living in sin just as much as He does now, and I am so glad that He wanted me, and when He found me, He was glad.

When I think of my daddy, I like to believe that he wanted me like Jesus did, but unlike Jesus, my daddy wasn't perfect. He was sick. He was an alcoholic, but I didn't know anything about alcoholism at that time, so I blamed my daddy and hated him for leaving me. I didn't know anything until he had passed on. I sometimes envision him holding me in his arms and telling me that he really did love me, and although I've made peace with him, it's still painful writing this because I still yearn to hear him say to me, "I love you, baby, and I'm sorry!"

The Value in the Valley by Iyanla Vanzant is one of my favorite books. A powerful quote from her book is, *"Life is an act of faith, and suffering is optional."* I didn't know that suffering was an option, and I definitely didn't know anything about faith. I suffered for many years mentally, spiritually, and physically while living each day by what I felt and saw. There are still times that I struggle usually when I'm refusing to accept things I cannot change or find the courage to change the things I can, but sometimes it can be hard turning things over to God even though I know I will gain peace and serenity by doing so. There are still times when I go to that place of fear and doubt, that room where the lights were turned off, and I would wake up in terror. The difference today is that I know that the light overcomes the darkness because John 1:5 (NIV) says that *"the light shines in the darkness and the darkness has not overcome it."* Praise God, I don't have to be afraid of the dark anymore!

I am patient with other women when they are still struggling with past issues that seem to be a really hard challenge for them, especially if they don't know the Lord because I myself went around and around in circles trying to get free, and I could find temporary freedom but not total freedom until I met God for myself. My twelve-step program definitely helped me to identify some of my issues by exposing them, and when I couldn't put any drugs on top of my pain, I had to humble myself to the God of my understanding. Year after year, working the steps kept me clean from drugs, but I wanted more than freedom from active addiction. I wanted to be more than clean. I wanted to be cleansed, and only the blood of Jesus was able to do that from the inside out. Hebrews 9:14 (NIV) says, *"How much more, then, will the blood of Christ who through the eternal Spirit offered himself unblemished to God, cleanse our consciences from acts that lead to death, so that we may serve the living God!"*

I was tormented in my mind, and I could not forget all the horrible things I had done to myself and others and all the things that had been done to me, and it was so hard trying to forgive myself no matter how many steps I had done. I absolutely hate the phrase "Just get over it" with a passion because it's just not that simple. It can take years and sometimes a lifetime to recover from trauma, and oftentimes many of us just learn how to cope with that little bit of pain that keeps coming back up every now and again, not to mention the memories. Hell, they don't ever go away! They hang around like a bad breakup, like when that dude left you at the abortion clinic with no money ten years ago, and you never got the chance to cuss him out. Now you're saved and saw him the other day in the grocery store—Jesus!

I will never forget how horrible those moments were and how afraid and hopeless I felt for so many years, but I have learned that we don't have to forget to be free, nor do we have to dismiss any of our life experiences. Instead, we should acknowledge that every part of us is important, and as horrible as things were in the past, I believe that everything happens for a reason, and the things that don't kill us will provide a valuable lesson. No matter how many valleys I find myself in today, I know there's something in it for me to learn. Like Iyanla says, *"There's value in the valley!"*

GRATITUDE SPEAKS

Happiness is not what brings us gratitude. It's gratitude that will bring us happiness.

Gratitude is an action. It affirms the greater good in the world and encourages us not only to appreciate gifts but to also repay them or pay them forward. I will be forever grateful for my family because they loved me even when I didn't have the ability to love myself and could not receive the love from them that they so desperately hoped would heal me. I am also grateful for my best friend of over twenty-six years, Tee, the godmother of my daughter and the person I called about everything, and even though she lived in Tennessee through the majority of my addiction while I, on the other hand, was a world traveler, she was always on the other end of that phone to encourage me and would come to my rescue at the drop of a dime ready to help me however she could.

I'm grateful to the many sponsors in my twelve-step program that have guided me through the steps and were willing to share their own personal experiences, strength, and hope, telling me that I didn't ever have to use again even if I wanted to. I am also grateful for the many sponsees who entrusted me with their most painful secrets and allowed me to identify with them. Thank you ladies for giving me a greater sense of responsibility and a love for sisterhood. My former roommates and confidantes, Renae and T-Bone, who are my sisters in and out of recovery, we lived together, cried together, struggled together, and rode together through rehab and transitional housing, and today they both own a piece of my heart and are still my girls.

I will always be grateful for Mister, who was there and who witnessed many years of my drug addiction. Mister was my rock and my ride or die through some of the hardest years of my life, and he never gave up on me no matter how hard it got. We met when my daughter was just a year old, and instantly, he fell head over heels for both of us. When I say that he was baby daddy for seventeen years, he was just that, daddy! Many people in Detroit thought Mister was my daughter's real father because this brother showed up and supported my baby as a real dad would. Mister kept food on the table, and he kept my daughter and me in the finest clothes. He hung in there through the years as I spent many of them in and out of drug rehab centers, not to mention the geographical changes I would make, moving from city to city, running from my addiction in hopes of changing myself, only to be disappointed by the outcome! That was my way of getting better, but the truth was that I was running from the one person I could never get away from—me—and every time I came back to Detroit, beat down worse than I was when I left, Mister was there to pick me up, and for that I am grateful.

I'm not sure if I'll ever be grateful for active addiction; however, I am grateful for the lessons I learned through the process. Being in active addiction was hard and scary, and on many days, I wanted to die, and I very well could have at the hands of a stranger. I am grateful that God didn't let the enemy steal the breath out of my body. In spite of my disobedience and ignorance, He still had mercy. I'm also grateful for the help I received from the many rehab centers that planted a seed in me by giving me information about this horrible disease that kept me in bondage.

There were many others on my journey that tried to help me get clean, like Kay B. She ran a transitional house in Macon, Georgia, and didn't know anything about me except that I was an addict. She opened her door and her heart to me and shared her family with and even allowed me to come back a couple of times after a relapse. I even stayed at her momma's house for a few days after one of my binges. Thank you, Kay B., for showing me love when I was unable to give it to myself. To my Uncle Pierre and his sweet wife, Dee, thank you for setting a plate at your table for me. I will treasure you both forever.

Auntie Eva was that auntie I could tell anything to, and she still is, and she tried her best to help me in every way she could and never shut her door on me or judged me for anything. There is nothing I would not do for her and my Uncle Cleve. I love you both to life every day.

For many years I lived in denial because I didn't know that I was lying to myself. Maybe it was just easier to make excuses instead of facing the truth, especially when I was still in shock and not sure what the real truth was, so using drugs and covering my feelings were just easier. I didn't know how to identify or express my feelings and emotions probably because I grew up in a time where you followed the rules, period, and a child's feelings didn't matter! I was taught by my mom at an early age to do what she said and not what she did. The problem was that I didn't know much of what she didn't do, and I couldn't hear what she was saying because my head was already filled with many other voices, but the things I witnessed her doing, like running away in the middle of the night from her ex-husband or fighting with her boyfriend, would train me up more than her words. Don't get me wrong, I adore my momma, but I was always afraid for her life, so I watched her more than I listened to her, and looking back today, I realize that most every fight and run were to protect us kids; and in spite of all her struggles, she kept a roof over our heads and food on the table, and I will be forever grateful for her, and I would lay down my life for her in a second!

I would be amiss if I didn't give a shoutout of gratitude to those practicing addicts that had grown up horribly in a way that I could never identify with but who saw some good in me and would shush me away, saying, "Go home, girl, you don't belong out in these streets. You better than this!" I couldn't understand how somebody so low, even lower than I was, could feel some compassion for me and give me a word of encouragement when I was feeling nothing but suicidal.

I believe that there were guardian angels sent by God to protect me. Even in the midst of my madness, God was there, saying, "I love you!" I knew there was something keeping me safe because on many occasions, death was all around me, and I escaped every time, like the time when I stole from a drug dealer, and he thought it was his nephew, so he put a hit out on his life. Another time, I went home with some guy I had never seen before only to find out that he was a total psychopath! I had to run for my life in the middle of the night as if I was trying to escape from Alcatraz. Then there were the many drug raids I found myself in and was shown grace again. There were police officers that would set me free in spite of the fact that I was guilty as sin. Thank you, Angel and Jerry D., for taking me in as your sister and loving me unconditionally. I didn't believe in unconditional love until I met you two! From the bottom of my heart, I will forever treasure our friendship.

Lord knows there were so many others that gave me grace and planted a seed of harvest in my life that would eventually grow up and change me for the better. The cries and stories that are shared in meetings from other addicts continue to give me empathy for other human beings that are suffering as I had been, not to mention the tears that are often evidence of many horrific experiences. Addicts have scars that are undetectable to the naked eye—there is no test or x-ray to establish where the bruises are, but believe me when I tell you there are many cuts and bruises. The twelve-step program gave me an open-door policy and a foundation that I could build upon, and on many days, it was a simple prayer or another addict in a meeting or on the other end of the phone that gave me the courage to stay clean one day at a time, and that kept me from losing my mind completely. The literature says that *we are threshed together*. The compassion and identification that we have for one another is priceless, and for this I am grateful.

JUST FOR TODAY

Just for today, I'm not quite where I want to be, but I'm not where I used to be, and at least I know I'm headed in the right direction. I question God today about things that I don't understand, and I know that God doesn't *make* bad things happen because the Bible says that God does not act wickedly. I live in recovery today, and I've experienced and seen so many miracles happen in my life and the lives of others, especially in the twelve-step program, where lives change for the better and success becomes the story of many recovering addicts.

Just for today, I know that I can't ever use any mind- or mood-altering substance, and I have accepted it, but there are times when I see someone drinking a glass of wine and seemingly enjoying life, and when I am offered a drink, sometimes I feel the need to explain why I must say no because of my own feelings of inadequacy, but I've learned to keep myself in safe environments as well as in a grateful state of mind, and I continue to remind myself that I have been set free from the need to be validated by others.

Just for today, I'm not angry about my past, but that doesn't mean I don't get angry because I do, just not for long periods. I also don't believe in mistakes. Instead, I believe we make choices, some for our benefit and others for our demise! I've learned that it's okay to speak my truth and move on in peace because anger has the ability to distort our thinking and change our behavior for the worst, which can cause us to become judgmental of others in spite of our own shortcomings and imperfections, which can be dangers both spiritually and physically. It's such a vicious cycle.

Just for today, I wanted those lost years back because I missed a lot of times with my daughter. I wanted to take my baby to Disney

World and see her eyes light up as a young child and to be there for every dance recital, but reality states that I can't get those years back; however, I can and I am the best parent I can be for her today, and I don't have to feel ashamed of the past. I found out that shame is just an emotion caused by a strong sense of guilt, embarrassment, unworthiness, disgrace, dishonor, condemnation, and disappointment, which I have also been set free of.

Just for today, I had to reconsider marriage, but I don't think God told me to leave my marriage. Instead, I think fear was so powerful in my life that it had become the thing I could hear the loudest, and running was my way of not dealing with the truth. When I got married, I was looking for a man that would fulfill my every need, and I did this full of anger and fear. I demanded my marriage and demeaned my husband all the way to the altar with my flawed character and defective personality. I can't tell you how this marriage will end, but I can tell you that my husband and I have become friends for the first time since we met, and we have also come to respect each other, which is a very important aspect in any relationship. I decided to stop trying to figure life out. Instead, I surrender my will daily by allowing God's will to be the author of my life.

Just for today, I believe that we all have our own personal demons, which could be different for each of us; for example, the way we think has the ability to destroy our lives if our thoughts are working against us and not modified! Our words and actions can cause disunity in our homes and relationships because words have the power to lift others up or tear them down! Our actions could affect our freedom, our present, and our future in one way or another. Our belief system is another factor that may cause us to remain unteachable and close-minded, which could definitely be classified as a form of bondage. The good news is that we have power over every wicked force by allowing others to assist us in our recovery whatever that means for the individual.

Just for today, I am grateful that I didn't die in active addiction because I would not be here to share with you that no matter what you are going through today, you can make it. A lot of things in my life is different with the help of a lot of people, but in the process of recovery, many have fallen off along the way, and there were many that did not understand my journey, and at first, it was a bit disappointing because I wanted all my friends and family to celebrate my new life, but everyone is not meant to enjoy our future. People show up in our lives for either a reason, a season, or a lifetime.

CHANGE

Every time you are tempted to react in the same old way, ask if you want to be a prisoner of the past or a pioneer of the future.

—Deepak Chopra

I've come to find that change makes no promises. It's either an act of pure faith or an unwillingness to move from one place to another. It is inevitable that change will happen, and it doesn't promise that your friends or family members will come along with you or even understand the process of change that happens in your life. To try and hold on to old relationships will force you to explain yourself again and again and will ultimately stunt your growth, leaving you defocused from the promises of God and your destiny, and without wisdom and understanding of how to navigate through this thing called life, you will sleep on your dreams.

The longer I stay clean, the more my friendship circle continues to change. In fact, it becomes smaller; however, my relationships are meaningful and of substance, which is very important to me. I need people in my life that can offer an exchange of positive energy because it's easy to get into negative thinking and speaking, but it's a process to get out of the cycle of negativity. I spent a lot of years thinking, speaking, and believing my negative thoughts especially about myself; therefore, it doesn't take much for my thinking to start going backward especially if I allow other people's negative words to get into my ears. I'm not saying that others can't come to me with problems—not at all. I love to be of service, but I need willingness and honesty to be present on both ends! I do understand when others are not ready or willing to make the sacrifice needed in order to change because change can be very uncomfortable. Besides, it took me a long time to be willing to do the work that brought about change. At one point in my life, I thought that the world needs to change in order for me to change, but that was so far from the truth. In fact, the change had to start within me because it was more about my perception and how I viewed the world than it was about what the world really was; therefore, when change began to happen within me, my perception of the world began to change. Today I live by the creed, "Let go and let God!"

FORGIVENESS

Forgiveness doesn't mean forgetting or excusing any harm done to us, and by no means do we have to make up with or break bread with the person who brought harm to us. However, forgiveness brings a kind of peace that helps us go on with life in a healthy fashion. To forgive someone is definitely a process. I know because it was and still is for me. I can tell you that for me it required making a decision, seeking guidance from a qualified therapist, and turning my will over to the care of God as I understood Him. I have forgiven my father for abandoning me because I know that he was sick. I do believe that he gave me what he had to offer. By doing so, I have been delivered from the resentment that I once held on to that would cause me to resent all men. There was a time when I went through the process of forgiving my aggressors, but I think that I am still in the process, so please forgive me if I need to take it one step and one day at a time.

LETTER TO MY DAD

Dear Dad, you never took time out for me. There were so many things I wanted to tell you. There were so many nights I went to bed in fear, wishing that you were there. I remember that picture of you all dressed up in your military suit. Your smile in that picture made me smile, and because I could never erase the memory of your face, every time I looked in the mirror, I saw your eyes in mine. There were so many things that I needed you for, not to mention the tears I cried that only one hug from you could have dried. I suffered for over twenty years with the same disease you had, and if I had only known about you, we could have helped each other, and maybe we wouldn't have felt so lost, different, and confused.

No one else in the family could understand me. They thought I was crazy, and I agreed with them because at one point I thought I was crazy too. I hated you for not being there to protect me from my abusers. If only you had been there, I know those men would have been afraid to even look my way, but you were MIA! They tormented not only my body but also my mind, leaving me embarrassed and guilty of a sin that I was innocent of. I allowed the abuse to define me by giving it the power to control my life for far too long.

Forgive me for the hate I felt in my heart for you, but you left me with no other choice! You left your little girl a fatherless daughter, and you never even got the chance to meet your granddaughter! She is amazing, and I know you would have loved her. I forgive you because I found out that forgiveness was not for you but for me, and as I forgave you, I made peace with my pain and begin to love and accept myself, and I found love and empathy for you as well.

I forgive you, Dad!

I have decided to make the rest of my life worth living on purpose by allowing a loving and caring God of my understanding to direct my path, and by His grace and mercy, I have found freedom from active addiction and from the secrets I kept!

ABOUT THE AUTHOR

My name is Kiva Crutcher. I grew up in the inner city of Detroit, Michigan, and I currently reside in the city of Murfreesboro, Tennessee. My husband is a twenty-year veteran, and my daughter is the product of my innermost strength and courage. Currently I am studying psychology in hopes of obtaining my master's in counseling. *The Secrets I Kept* is my personal journey of healing from addiction caused by childhood trauma. My innermost desire is to assist others who may be struggling with trauma and substance-use disorder through their own personal journey of recovery.

Printed in the USA
CPSIA information can be obtained
at www.ICGtesting.com
LVHW090236091024
793326LV00002B/273

9 798889 825951